T0043500

Meeting
Muhammad

OMAR SULEIMAN

KUBE
PUBLISHING

In association with

YAQEEN
INSTITUTE FOR ISLAMIC RESEARCH

Meeting Muhammad ﷺ

First published in England by
Kube Publishing Ltd
Markfield Conference Centre
Ratby Lane, Markfield
Leicestershire, LE67 9SY
United Kingdom

Tel: +44 (0) 1530 249230

Website: www.kubepublishing.com
Email: info@kubepublishing.com

Cataloguing-in-Publication Data is available from the
British Library.

ISBN 978-1-84774-177-6 Casebound
eISBN 978-1-84774-178-3 Ebook

Proofreading and editing: Wordsmiths
Cover design, Arabic calligraphy and typesetting: Jannah Haque
Printed by: IMAK Ofset, Turkey.

Transliteration Guide

A brief guide to some of the letters and symbols used in the Arabic transliteration in this book.

th	ث	*ḥ*	ح	*dh*	ذ
ṣ	ص	*ḍ*	ض	*ṭ*	ط
ẓ	ظ	ʿ	ع	ʾ	ء

ā	ـَا آ	*ī*	ـِي	*ū*	ـُو

May the peace and blessings of Allah be upon him.

Glorified and Majestic (is He).

May Allah be pleased with him.

May Allah be pleased with her.

May Allah be pleased with them both.

May peace be upon him.

May peace be upon her.

May peace be upon them both.

Contents

Introduction

Ḥassān ibn Thābit ☙ once paid homage to the Prophet ﷺ by reciting the following words:

وَأَحْسَنُ مِنْكَ لَمْ تَرَ قَطُّ عَيْنِي

"My eyes have never seen anything better than you...

وَأَجْمَلُ مِنْكَ لَمْ تَلِدِ النِّسَاءُ

No woman has ever
given birth to anyone
as beautiful as you...

خُلِقْتِ مُبَرّاءً مِنْ كُلِّ عَيْبٍ

*You were
created free from
all flaws...*

كَأَنَّكَ قَدْ خُلِقْتَ كَمَا تَشَاء

*As if you
were created exactly
as you wished."*

Despite having such beautiful appearance, the Prophet's character was in fact even more striking and beautiful. Had you been given the opportunity to observe his conduct in person, you would have most definitely stated the words of ʿAlī ﷺ:

لَمْ أَرَ قَبْلَهُ وَلَا بَعْدَهُ مِثْلَهُ

"I have never seen anyone like him,
whether before or after him."

Had you lived in his time, you would have longed to see him each and every day. You would have immensely enjoyed his smiles, speeches, and recreational activities with children, regardless of whether these children were his or yours. Furthermore, you would have loved to pray behind him, observe days of fasting with him, and celebrate the days of Eid in his presence. Likewise, you would have considered him to be a wise teacher and noble friend at the same time. You would have taken the initiative to host him in your residence, so that you could serve him food and hold private conversations with him. As later members of this *ummah*, we can only rely on the narrations transmitted to us in order to appreciate and perceive what it meant to be one of his Companions in this world. By examining these narrations, not only does our love for him increase, but we also long to be from among his Companions in the next world.

In this book, we embark upon a noble journey in which we move on from simply knowing the Prophet ﷺ to actually loving him and developing a spiritual connection with him. May our hearts long for the love and company of the Beloved. *Āmīn*.

May the peace
and blessings of Allah
be upon him.

1

His Appearance

It is reported that Qatādah ﷺ said:

مَا بَعَثَ اللهُ نَبِيًّا إِلَّا حَسَنَ الوَجْهِ حَسَنَ الصَّوتِ

"Allah never sent a Prophet except that they were characterised with a beautiful face and voice."

In the case of the Prophet ﷺ, the Companions never witnessed any person or thing which was as beautiful as him, whether before or after Islam. While it is true that many people can have a beautiful external appearance but be blemished with bad character traits, the case of the Prophet ﷺ was completely different. This was because while his physical composition was of utmost beauty, his internal character traits—which Allah praised him for—were in fact even more beautiful.

'Abdullāh ibn Rawāḥah ﷺ once described the presence of the Prophet ﷺ in a vivid manner by saying:

لَو لَم تَكُن فِيهِ آيَاتٌ مُبَيَّنَةٌ
كَانَت بَدِيهَتُهُ تُنبِيكَ بِالخَبَرِ

*"If the Prophet ﷺ did not say anything and had
nothing except his presence, you would still be
able to discern a divine beauty within him."*

Thus we come across many stories where people would embrace Islam just by looking at the Prophet ﷺ. For instance, 'Abdullāh ibn Salām ﷺ presided as the head rabbi of Madinah before the Prophet migrated to the city. Upon the Prophet's arrival, he went out to see him in person. He did not have to even listen to the Prophet's speech to know his truthfulness and sincerity. For as he stated, "I looked at his face, and I knew that this is not the face of a liar *(laysa bi-wajh kadhdhāb)*."

The Prophet's physical attributes are outlined in elaborate detail in the *shamā'il* genre, which refers to the corpus of works that study the description of the Prophet ﷺ. Within the reports related to this field, it is common to find hadiths which describe the Prophet ﷺ as being more beautiful than the moon. One hadith in this regard states:

كَانَ رَسُوْلُ اللهِ صَلَّى اللهُ عَلَيهِ وَسَلَّمَ فَخْمًا مُفَخَّمًا، يَتَلَأْلَأُ وَجْهُهُ،
تَلَأْلُؤَ الْقَمَرِ لَيْلَةَ الْبَدْرِ

*"The Prophet ﷺ had an awe-inspiring appearance.
His face was more radiant and beautiful than the full
moon on the darkest of nights."*

One can appreciate the full force of this report once
they realise how awesome and awe-inspiring the full
moon appears in the desert climate. Furthermore, one
is also amazed when reading the following report of
Anas ibn Mālik ﷺ, who stated: "One night I tried to
compare the moon with the face of the Prophet ﷺ, and
asked myself: which one of the two is more radiant?
Upon reflection, I came to the realisation that the face
of the Prophet ﷺ is more radiant and beautiful than
the full moon in the desert." This is despite the fact
that the full moon is not just immensely beautiful, but
it is also fully captivating; if someone is outside, they
cannot look at anything besides it.

As for his other physical characteristics, they were
perfectly harmonious and balanced. Recall how Allah
describes Jibrīl ﷺ coming to Maryam ﷺ in the form
of a perfectly symmetrical man (*basharan sawiyyan*).[1]
In the case of the Prophet ﷺ, everything in his body
was perfectly shaped and fashioned. He was not too tall,

---

1   *Maryam*, 17.

nor was he short. His skin colour was not too light, nor was it too dark. He was described as being *azhar al-lawn*, meaning he had a bright skin colour. However, at the same time, his skin colour was not pale white. His face was not too round, nor was it too narrow, but it was closer to the former. Now, imagine that you are standing in front of the Prophet ﷺ, and have the chance to look directly at his face. What would draw your attention first? According to Umm Maʿbad ؓ, the eyes of the Prophet ﷺ were of a perfect contrast, as the sclera found in his eyes was extremely white, while his pupils were intensely black. His eyelashes were so long that one would assume that they always had antimony (*kuḥl*) applied on them. His eyes were always moist due to the tears that they would shed. He also had thick and curved eyebrows which were on the verge of connecting, but they were separated by a small space. On this line of separation the light would beautifully shine. Furthermore, he was described as having a prominent forehead (*ʿaẓīm al-hāmah*), upon which a vein would appear only if he ever became upset. His nose was neither flat nor pointy, but it was perfectly sloped. It also was blessed with a specific shining light that made it appear relatively large for an onlooker. However, if one came closer to the presence of the Prophet ﷺ, they realised that it was the glimmer of light which made his nose more prominent.

The blessed teeth of the Prophet ﷺ would appear when he opened his mouth to speak. The Companions described his teeth as being white as hailstones and perfectly aligned. This is no matter of surprise, as the Prophet ﷺ frequently cleaned his teeth with the tooth-stick (*siwāk*), using it at least five times for the daily prayers. His teeth were not fused or joined together; rather, each tooth was neatly separated with a fine and even line of separation. His mouth was wide. He ﷺ was known to articulate his statements in a clear and crisp manner, such that every pronounced word was heard with ease. His voice was characterised with a beautiful melodious rhythm which imparted a natural echo. His hair, just like in the case of everything else was perfectly balanced, being neither straight nor curly. Instead, it was a wavy form of hair. In some cases, the Prophet ﷺ would let it grow to his earlobes, and in other circumstances he would leave it until it descended to his shoulders. However, it is true that when performing Hajj or 'Umrah, he would shave his head. The Prophet ﷺ also was noted to have a full and thick beard, which he would regularly comb and treat well. Throughout most of his life, the hairs of his beard were fully black. After his death, the Companions only found a low range of 14 to 20 grey hairs in both his head and beard. This was despite the fact that the Prophet ﷺ passed away at the age of 63. Most of these hairs were found right under his lips,

Anas ibn Mālik ﷺ stated: "One night I tried to compare the moon with the face of the Prophet ﷺ, and asked myself: which one of the two is more radiant? Upon reflection, I came to the realisation that the face of the Prophet ﷺ is more radiant and beautiful than the full moon in the desert."

and on his sideburns. In fact, the Companions noted that when the Prophet ﷺ used oil to treat his hair, the grey hairs were no longer visible.

The Prophet's neck was long, beautiful, and elegant. It had the slender beauty of a gazelle's neck. As for his shoulders, chest, and arms, they were all strong and broad. Until the day of his death, his stomach did not extend beyond his chest, which means that he maintained a stable weight and fitness. With the exception of his face and head, the Prophet ﷺ did not have much hair on the rest of the body. He only had a thin line of hair on his chest that ran all the way down to his navel. The Prophet ﷺ was described as having large, well-defined, and well-fortified limbs. He thus had large bones, hands, and feet. He ﷺ likewise had large and perfectly-round calves, but had absolutely no weight on his heels. His lower body was said to be so strong that he could easily mount his riding animal without the use of any saddle. This is why one will find al-Ḥasan ﷺ being described as resembling the Prophet ﷺ in his upper body—meaning in terms of beauty. Al-Ḥusayn ﷺ, on the other hand, was said to resemble his grandfather in having a similar lower body structure. This is because al-Ḥusayn ﷺ was a powerful and formidable warrior. Despite the size and strength of his limbs, Anas ibn Mālik ﷺ said that the Prophet's limbs were smoother than silk, and water would slither right off them.

He ﷺ likewise had a beautiful natural scent, and
his body would exude sweat which smelled like
an elegant form of perfume. Those who shook his
hand testified that the pleasant smell from it would
remain on their own hands for days. Even his blessed
mouth exuded a pleasant breath. Anyone who saw
him from afar would testify how his appearance
would strike and captivate them. If he ﷺ came close
to someone, his beauty was so overwhelming that
a person could not stare at him directly. Al-Barā'
narrated that one night he saw the Prophet ﷺ, who
was on this particular occasion wearing a red Yemeni
garment (*ḥullah*). After seeing the Prophet ﷺ in this
dress, al-Barā' said: "I have never seen a sight more
beautiful than the Prophet ﷺ on that night." On a
similar note, Abū Hurayrah said: "Whenever I saw
the Prophet ﷺ, his body was so perfectly set that
it was as if he was moulded in silver." Without any
doubt, the most famous thing about the Prophet ﷺ
was his smile. He ﷺ was known to always have a
smile on his face, regardless of whether he ﷺ was in a
state of happiness or sadness. Regarding this matter,
Ka'b ibn Mālik said: "When he ﷺ was in a happy
mood (*idhā surra*), his face would become even more
radiant." Yet, we should ask how it was possible that
the Prophet ﷺ was always smiling, since he ﷺ was
also described as being in a state of grief (*mutawāṣil
al-aḥzān*), deep state of contemplation (*dā'im al-fikr*),

and never allowed himself to rest during his life. He ﷺ was always carrying a heavy burden in order to protect and raise his *ummah*. This apparent contradiction can be explained by looking at an important point regarding etiquette which Allah describes in the Qur'an. Some people might appear to be well-off and free of problems, but that is only because of how they are able to carry their burdens. Related to this point, smiling is an act of charity (*ṣadaqah*), and the Prophet ﷺ smiled towards members of his *ummah* as an act of generosity and in order to bring joy to their hearts. But at the same time, he would intensely weep to his Lord and pray for the joy and success of his *ummah*. Thus, the Prophet combined two great qualities which indicated his intense love for his *ummah*. There was no man that smiled more for his *ummah* than the Prophet ﷺ, and at the same there was no person who cried more for his *ummah* than the Prophet ﷺ.

Smiling is an act of charity and so the Prophet ﷺ smiled towards members of his ummah as an act of generosity to bring joy to their hearts. However, he would also intensely weep to his Lord and pray for the joy and success of his ummah. Thus, he combined two great qualities which indicated his intense love for his ummah.

2

His Blessed Demeanour

With reference to character, there are many verses of the Qur'an which emphasise subtle etiquettes pertaining to body language. In fact, when Allah ﷻ describes the qualities of His elite class of believers (*'ibād al-Raḥmān*), the first thing He mentions about them is their demeanour in terms of how they tread the earth lightly:

وَعِبَادُ الرَّحْمَنِ الَّذِينَ يَمْشُونَ عَلَى الأَرْضِ هَوناً

"The servants of the Most Compassionate are those who walk on the earth humbly..." [2]

Likewise, when Luqmān al-Ḥakīm ﷺ was giving his son advice, he emphasised the importance of speaking and walking in a dignified manner. Furthermore, when

---

[2] *al-Furqān*, 63.

Allah discusses how we should respond to our
parents, we are told not to grunt to them by saying
even "*uff*". These points are also emphasised in
the Prophet's statements as well. For example, in
one hadith he said that a person should not be
treacherous with their eyes. This prohibits one from
winking and making inappropriate facial expressions
behind someone's back in a way that betrays them.
When we evaluate the Prophet's body language
and demeanour, we will realise that all their facets
embody his universal message.

First and foremost, you might be surprised to find
someone so beautiful to be so shy and bashful. But it
was our own Prophet who once emphasised how
shyness (*ḥayā'*) constitutes a key quality (*khuluq*)
of our religion. In one important hadith, he said:
"Every religion has its distinct characteristic, and
the distinct characteristic of Islam is modesty." Our
Prophet was the most shy and bashful of people,
despite his well-known eminent rank and possession
of supreme traits.

But what was his demeanour and character like?
We already pointed out previously that he would
constantly smile. In one report, he is described as
being both *bassām* and *ḍaḥḥāk*, which means that
he was one who intensively smiled and caused

others to smile; he ﷺ often laughed and caused others to laugh as well.

But his laughter was always done in a dignified and well-composed manner. In reality, his laugh was actually a wide smile, where his mouth would open to the extent that his back teeth would become visible. Even the occasions when he ﷺ laughed reveals many insights into his character. He ﷺ would laugh when others would laugh or be in a cheerful mood. But he would also laugh by widening his smile whenever Allah gave him good news. 'Alī ibn Abī Ṭālib ﷺ mentions that the Prophet ﷺ would express joy and laughter after concluding an act of worship (*ʿibādah*). He would also laugh whenever he would share narrations about Allah's infinite mercy, such as the narration of the last man who will enter Paradise. This man will think that Allah ﷻ is mocking him because he does not fathom the scope of Allah's mercy and generosity. The Prophet ﷺ laughed when relating this narration, and said: "Allah ﷻ laughs at that man when the man said, 'O Allah, are you making fun of me? And you are the Lord of the world.'" It should be noted that his laugh was not audible, but it was clearly distinct from his customary smile, as his back teeth would be visible.

The Prophet ﷺ was also noted for occasionally observing long periods of silence. Sometimes, when a person is endowed with beauty, eloquence, and power, they often dominate every single conversation or gathering. The Prophet ﷺ would largely maintain silence so that he could be in a state of reflection. At the same time, however, he ﷺ was known to be deeply perceptive. During these gatherings, he ﷺ would only speak a limited number of words which were proportionate to the size of the congregation. He ﷺ was endowed with the priceless gift of coherent language (*ḥulw al-manṭiq*), where he ﷺ would always speak in a beautiful and logical manner. He ﷺ would directly address the point of contention when speaking. As noted before, his articulation was crisp and coherent. In order to ensure that a point was understood and absorbed by his audience, he ﷺ would speak slowly and repeat himself. That way, members of his audience would immediately understand his reminders and admonitions.

Despite his beauty, the Prophet would often keep his gaze lowered. When he ﷺ looked at people he was addressing, he ﷺ would not stare for long periods, but would only glance momentarily, and then look down. That was due to his beautiful humility. But if he ﷺ noticed that you enjoyed his eye contact, he would not break it. If he observed that one was at awe due to his

*W*hen being addressed by someone, the Prophet ﷺ would not just turn his head towards the speaker. He ﷺ would make that person the centre of attention by turning his entire body towards them.

beautiful gaze, then he ✽ would look away. This is a reflection of how powerful and striking his gaze was. ʿAmr ibn al-ʿĀṣ said: "If you ask me to describe the Prophet, I would not be able to do so. This is because even though I was in front of him, I could not look up at him due to my reverence and admiration for him (ijlālan wa taʿẓīmān)."

When being addressed by someone, the Prophet ✽ would not just turn his head towards the speaker. He ✽ would make that person the centre of attention by turning his entire body towards them, to let them know that he ✽ was fully listening to what they had to say. If one had a request, he ✽ would immediately lend them his ear and not remove his attention until that person finished mentioning what they had to say. If someone shook his hand, the Prophet ✽ would not remove his hand until that person first removed theirs. This was to indicate to the other side that he ✽ was ready to speak with them or listen to anything they had to say.

I would like to share one of my favourite narrations about the Prophet ✽ in this regard. It has serious consequences for us today, especially with our obsession with cellphones. The Prophet ✽ had a silver ring containing an Abyssinian ruby stone, which he adored and often wore. The Prophet ✽ once looked at his ring a few times in the middle of a conversation. He ultimately became disappointed with himself ﷺ simply due to being distracted by his ring while speaking with his Companions. So he actually took off this ring and cast it aside. He explained that he did this because he found it to be diverting himself from the words of his Companions. When he ﷺ wanted to refer to a person, he would not point with a single finger, since that usually has a negative accusatory connotation to it. Instead, he ﷺ would only point with his entire hand, so the referred person would not feel or believe that they are being reproached.

When the Prophet ﷺ would become amazed or pleased by an amusing piece of information, he would tap his thigh and exclaim, "*Subḥānallāh!*" When the Prophet ﷺ would walk, he would do so like a person with a strong sense of purpose. ʿAlī ﷺ said that the Prophet's walking was like a man walking downhill. In addition, Abū Hurayrah ﷺ mentioned that the Prophet ﷺ would walk in a brisk manner, such that one could not keep up with his pace. He ﷺ was always motivated to do good and determined to be productive. He ﷺ did not walk in an arrogant or lazy manner.

He ﷺ also exhibited humility and simplicity in his manner of sitting. Allah sent an angel to the Prophet ﷺ and gave him the choice of whether he would prefer to be a prophet-king (*nabiyy malik*) or a prophet-slave (*nabiyy ʿabd*). If he ﷺ chose the former position, he could live as a ruling king, but still serve as a prophet. But the Prophet ﷺ chose to live as a humble slave, and he ﷺ mentioned that is why he would always sit up while eating his food. He ﷺ refused to recline his back, which was the conduct of the wealthy, arrogant, or ruling people.

So everything that the Prophet ﷺ did in his daily conduct and demeanour reflected his supreme humility, modesty, sincerity to Allah, and service to the people.

3

Attending His Khuṭbah

A way to familiarise ourselves with the Prophet ﷺ on a personal level can be by discussing his delivery of the Friday prayer (*Ṣalāh al-Jumuʿah*). I want you to imagine that you are in the Prophet's *masjid* in Madinah on a Friday, and you are waiting for him to ascend the pulpit (*minbar*) and deliver the weekly sermon (*khuṭbah*). What state is your heart in? How excited are you to listen to him? And how are you going to be looking at him when he delivers the sermon?

The Prophet ﷺ taught us to treat Friday like a special occasion. He ﷺ is reported to have said:

إِنَّ هَذَا يَوْمٌ جَعَلَهُ اللهُ عِيدًا لِلْمُسْلِمِينَ، فَمَنْ جَاءَ إِلَى الْجُمُعَةِ فَلْيَغْتَسِلْ، وَإِنْ كَانَ طِيبٌ فَلْيَمَسَّ مِنْهُ، وَعَلَيْكُمْ بِالسِّوَاكِ

"This day is a festival that Allah has ordained for the Muslims. Whoever comes to the Friday prayer,

let them take a bath (ghusl). And if he has some
perfume, then let him put some on. And use the
tooth-stick (siwāk)."

The Prophet ﷺ would ensure that he implemented
these pieces of advice himself. Before coming to the
Friday prayer, he ﷺ would make sure to perform a
bath just beforehand, so his body would be fresh
and clean. He ﷺ would put on his best perfume, and
ensure that it was applied on every part of his body.
He ﷺ would also have a fresh tooth-stick, which he
would use to clean his teeth. He ﷺ would wear his
best clothes on two particular occasions. One of
them was whenever he ﷺ would receive a delegation.
The second case was whenever he ﷺ would deliver
the Friday sermon. On one occasion, ʿUmar ibn
al-Khaṭṭāb ﷺ saw a beautiful silk garment in the
market, and he decided to purchase it so the Prophet ﷺ
could wear it on those two special occasions. So he
bought it and presented it to the Prophet as a gift.
The Prophet ﷺ thanked him for the offering, but
ultimately declined by noting that such garments are
impermissible for the Muslims. So ʿUmar said: "I
took that silk robe and gave it to one of my brothers,
who had not accepted Islam yet." The Prophet ﷺ
said: "If anyone among you can afford to buy a pair
of garments for Friday besides their work clothes,
then let them do so if it is feasible (*in wajada saʿah*)."

*T*he Prophet ﷺ stopped his sermon, descended from the pulpit, and picked up his little grandchildren al-Ḥusayn and al-Ḥasan ﷺ. He made duʿāʾ for both of them, and then had them sit on his lap while he returned to the pulpit.

After entering the *masjid* on Fridays, the Prophet ﷺ would ascend the pulpit, and then give his greetings to the congregation. He ﷺ would then sit, with a staff in his hand. Then Bilāl ؓ would stand and give the call to prayer (*adhān*). People in that time would not prioritise sitting near or against the walls, which is commonly done today. Instead, they followed what was prescribed by the Prophet ﷺ:

أُحْضُرُوا الذِّكْرَ وَادْنُوا مِنَ الإِمَامِ فَإِنَّ الرَّجُلَ لَا يَزَالُ يَتَبَاعَدُ حَتَّى يُؤَخَّرَ فِي الْجَنَّةِ وَإِنْ دَخَلَهَا

"Attend the sermon and sit close to the Imam. For a man keeps himself away until he will be left behind at the time of entering Paradise, though he eventually enters it."

While it is true that people should gather around and get as close as possible to the Imam, this does not permit one to cross over or around people. When people tried to do such things, the Prophet ﷺ would order them to desist from doing so and instead asked them to sit in their place. On one occasion, the Prophet ﷺ had started delivering his sermon, and a man entered the congregation and tried to cross through the lines of people to get closer to the Prophet ﷺ. The Prophet ﷺ noticed this, and addressed the man by stating:

اِجْلِسْ؛ فَقَدْ آذَيْتَ وَآنَيْتَ

*"Sit down, for you have both harmed the people
and come late."*

What is immensely fascinating about the Prophet ﷺ
is that during the sermon he was able to carefully
observe the state of the entire setting and congregation,
and would take measures if the circumstances called
for them. As Abū Qays ﷺ interestingly notes in one
narration: "I came to the *masjid*, and the Prophet ﷺ
was delivering the sermon. So I stood listening to him,
while being under the sun's light. The Prophet ﷺ
motioned to me to sit in a shaded area instead."
Likewise, there is the story of Sulayk al-Ghaṭafānī ﷺ,
who entered the *masjid* on a Friday and sat without
praying. The Prophet paused his sermon, and ordered
him to stand and pray two *rak'ahs*. Some versions of the
narration suggest that the Prophet ﷺ ordered Sulayk
to pray during the sermon so all the congregants
would notice his dire state of poverty. That way, they
would be moved to donate to him after the prayer,
without there being any need for him to directly ask or
beg. So the Prophet ﷺ was able to maintain command
of the room while standing over the pulpit.

There is also a moving story relating to al-Ḥusayn
and al-Ḥasan ﷺ, who once ran towards to the
Prophet ﷺ while he was standing and delivering the

sermon over the pulpit. During this episode, they were both little children, wearing beautiful red garments. They both tried to hastily run towards the Prophet ☀, but kept tripping over their own garments. One could imagine how much this scene garnered the attention of everyone in the audience. Upon noticing this, the Prophet stopped his sermon, descended from the pulpit, and picked up both al-Ḥusayn and al-Ḥasan ☀. He then recited the verse:

إِنَّمَا أَمْوَالُكُمْ وَ أَوْلَادُكُمْ فِتْنَةٌ

"Your wealth and children are only a test (fitnah)." [3]

He made *duʿāʾ* for both of them, and then had them sit on his lap while he returned to the pulpit.

How was the sermon of the Prophet ☀? Imagine that you are sitting before him on Friday, while he is in full command of the room. You will undoubtedly be in full awe of him, as the Prophet would be in his best appearance, while wearing the most beautiful of clothing. Furthermore, you will likewise be moved by his firm reminders regarding life and death. There is a very fascinating narration from Umm Hishām ☀ — the daughter of al-Ḥārith ibn Nuʿmān—which pertains to this issue. She interestingly noted: "I memorised

---

[3] *al-Taghābun*, 15.

The Prophet ﷺ often used parables and aphorisms (amthāl) in his sermons to ensure his audience fully understood his reminders. He ﷺ was described as being deeper and more eloquent than the breadth of an ocean.

Surah Qāf directly from the mouth of the Prophet 襲 simply by attending his Friday sermons." This is because he 襲 used to recite and explain this surah every single week. The reason why this chapter was given so much attention in particular is because it discusses life and death in extensive detail.

The Companions would listen to the Prophet's sermons with their hearts open, and their minds fully tranquil. They would listen attentively to his sermons regarding life and death, and their bodies were so still that it was as if there were birds on top of their heads. This vivid description indicates how still they remained throughout the Prophet's reminder.

To make his sermons more effective, the Prophet 襲 used his hands in order to gesture, motion, and describe the topics he sought to address. His words were crisp and articulate, and to ensure his points were fully understood, he would sometimes repeat the same sentence three times. His eyes and tone of voice would neatly correspond with the topic he was talking about. For instance, if he 襲 was speaking about something pleasing which induced happiness, you would be able to detect emotions denoting cheerfulness from his tone and eyes. Conversely, if he 襲 spoke of something which induced anger or sadness, the same feelings could be detected in his eyes and tone.

He ﷺ would use his hands as teaching implements to effectively deliver his points. When he described the believers as being a building, he ﷺ would firmly clench his hands together to indicate their accumulated strength. When he ﷺ warned about the tongue's dangers, he ﷺ pointed towards his mouth. In addition, when speaking about the opening of the doors of Paradise (*Jannah*), he ﷺ made the hand motion for opening its door. He ﷺ would often point to the heavens as well.

Likewise, the Prophet ﷺ often used parables and aphorisms (*amthāl*) to ensure his audience fully understood his reminders. He ﷺ was described as being deeper and more eloquent than the breadth of an ocean. When analysing the Prophet's skills as an orator, we must consider a few basic facts. This is the most recorded man in history, with thousands of his statements fully documented and compiled. Yet, when imparting his eloquent sayings, the Prophet ﷺ never had to use prepared speeches or cues. He ﷺ simply delivered his statements directly from the heart, and reminded people of their obligations. The Companions knew of his status and his pure sincerity, which made his statements even more moving and effective.

Nowadays, the sound system in the *masjid* goes out due to lapses in technology or electricity. But in the

Prophet's time, the sound system once failed for another reason. Asmā' bint Abī Bakr ﷺ mentioned that on a particular Friday the women could not listen to the Prophet's sermon, since the male Companions in front of them were intensely crying. This stoked their interest on what caused the male Companions to cry so much. After the prayer, they stopped the men and asked them what caused them to become so emotional. They responded by stating that the Prophet ﷺ was speaking about the trials and tribulations of the grave.

4

Praying Behind Him

Imam al-Ḥasan al-Baṣrī ﷺ once eloquently stated,

الصَّلَاةُ مِعْرَاجُ المُؤْمِنِ

"The prayer is the ascent of the believer."

What the Imam meant by this statement is that you directly connect with Allah ﷻ during prayer. You even spiritually ascend in a way which resembles the divine night when the Prophet ﷺ received the order to pray while he was in the heavens. That was none other than the divine night journey (*al-Isrāʾ wa al-Miʿrāj*). So prayer is a very intimate and powerful experience. Of course, we have somewhat lost this experience ever since being deprived of performing the prayer in congregation behind an Imam with a beautiful voice inside our local *masjids*.

But how did it feel to perform the five daily prayers behind the Prophet ﷺ, who was the one who received the command of prayer from Allah directly? The Prophet ﷺ would come out to lead the prayer, and he recited the Qur'an in a very particular way. Of course, he ﷺ was the one who received the Qur'an, so his recitation would obviously be characterised with a unique quality. Likewise, this naturally meant that he ﷺ would confer the prayer specific importance, and give every *rak'ah* and motion specific attention. People who prayed behind him testified to how perfect and tranquil his prayer was.

But how was his recitation? The Prophet ﷺ had an exceptionally beautiful voice. Recall what Qatādah ﵁ beautifully observed:

مَا بَعَثَ اللّٰهُ نَبِيًّا إِلَّا حَسَنَ الوَجْهِ حَسَنَ الصَّوتِ

"Allah never sent a Prophet except that they were characterised with a beautiful face and voice."

Regarding his recitation, the Companions state:

كَانَ يُقَطِّعُ قِراءَتَهُ آيةً آيةً

"When he would recite the Qur'an, he was known to pause between the verses, reciting them one by one."

Furthermore, he ﷺ used to deliver his recitation in a crisp and clear manner. Just like how the Prophet ﷺ used to speak slowly and articulate his words clearly, likewise his recitation of the Qur'an was steady, and every verse was recited separately. His voice also had a beautiful natural melody, but the volume of his recitation was not too loud. It was loud enough for one to hear him during the congregation; if you were near his house, you would be able to hear his recitation from his house's courtyard.

Now it is known that the Prophet ﷺ would frequently get emotional while reciting. However, the way the Prophet ﷺ would cry during his recitation was unique and restrained. They described the Prophet's crying during his recitation as being a form of humming from the chest, which resembled the sound of a boiling kettle pot. This is very similar to how the Prophet's laughter was inaudible, but instead more of a wider smile. Likewise, his weeping was done in a controlled and dignified manner, as it was done quietly. Yet it was purely sincere, and one could tell that these emotions were coming directly from the heart.

His eyes used to shed tears profusely while reciting or listening to the Qur'an. In fact, he ﷺ would shed tears even if he ﷺ did not make any sound of weeping. ʿAbdullāh ibn Masʿūd ﷺ mentions that he was once asked by the Prophet to recite the Qur'an in front of him. In response, Ibn Mas'ūd ﷺ said:

يَا رَسُولَ اللهِ كَيْفَ أَقْرَأُ عَلَيْكَ وَإِنَّمَا أُنْزِلَ عَلَيْكَ

"O Messenger of Allah! You want me to recite the Qur'an, while it was revealed to you?"

The Prophet said: "I would love to hear it from someone else besides me." He said: "So I recited *Surah al-Nisā'* and then I reached the verse,

فَكَيْفَ إِذَا جِئْنَا مِن كُلِّ أُمَّةٍ بِشَهِيدٍ وَجِئْنَا بِكَ عَلَى هَـؤُلَاءِ شَهِيدًا

'So how will it be when We bring a witness from every faith-community and bring you as a witness against yours?'[4]

Upon hearing this verse, the Prophet ﷺ put his hand on my thigh and said: 'Enough (*ḥasbuk*).'" Ibn Mas'ūd looked up and realised that the Prophet's eyes were flowing with tears, and were like faucets. He did not notice this because the Prophet ﷺ never wept loudly; instead he would cry sincerely and quietly, such that no one would notice his emotional state.

The attentive state of his heart caused his eyes to always be moist and tearful. Now, the Prophet ﷺ

---

[4] *al-Nisā'*, 41.

would always be spiritually connected with Allah in his daily prayers, whether obligatory or voluntary. But the Prophet ﷺ would never cause himself to get carried away with his prayers while leading, lest he ﷺ overburden his followers. Regarding this matter, he said that when one leads the obligatory prayers (*farā'iḍ*), they should keep them short. This is because in the congregation there are the elderly, the sick, women that come with their children, and those who have to run errands. This means that the prayer of the Prophet ﷺ was relatively short whenever he was leading the obligatory prayer. In fact, if the Prophet ﷺ heard a child cry during the prayer, he would not reprimand the parents after the conclusion of the prayer. Instead, he would speed up his recitation and other parts of the prayer, as he understood the difficulties that parents and grandparents would experience in such circumstances.

There were in fact circumstances when al-Ḥusayn and al-Ḥasan ﷺ—particularly al-Ḥasan—would jump on the Prophet's back during his obligatory prayer, whenever he descended into prostration (*sajdah*). The Prophet ﷺ would wait for them to come off his back before rising, so that they would not be harmed.

Likewise, Umāmah ﷺ would come to the Prophet ﷺ as a baby girl while he was praying. The Prophet ﷺ

The Prophet's ﷺ little grandchildren, al-Ḥusayn and al-Ḥasan ﷺ would jump on his back during his prayer when he descended into prostration (sajdah). He would wait for them to come off his back before rising to avoid any harm. He would carry his baby granddaughter, Umāmah ﷺ while leading the prayer, gently putting her down when descending to prostrate.

would carry her in his arms while he led the prayer, and would gently put her down whenever descending to prostrate. So his obligatory prayer was always beautiful to follow, and you would discern his pure sincerity and pleasant recitation, despite these sessions being relatively short.

But what about the voluntary prayer? We can understand the important of voluntary prayers, as we are currently in the month of Ramadan and long for performing the *tarāwīḥ* prayers as we did before the COVID-19 crisis. This love for the *tarāwīḥ* prayers was even found among the Companions, as they would congregate in the *masjid* and longed to listen to the Prophet's recitation of the Qur'an during the nights of Ramadan. The *masjid* would become so full such that it could not even hold all the attendees. The Prophet ﷺ eventually ceased these congregational sessions, as he did not want the *tarāwīḥ* prayer to become obligatory (*farḍ*) upon the people.

Zayd ibn Thābit ﷺ has a very fascinating narration regarding this matter. He mentions that the Prophet had set up a chamber in his *masjid*, and would offer his night vigil prayers (*qiyām*) in that particular location. When the people found out about the Prophet's practice, they informed one another about it and began praying behind him. On the nights that the Prophet ﷺ would not come, they would cough, go out of his door, raise their voices slightly, and even throw some pebbles in the direction of his house in order to draw his attention. This was all done out of the hope that the Prophet ﷺ would hear them, come out, and lead them in prayer. Eventually, the Prophet ﷺ exited his house one night and appeared before them. He was visibly upset. He ﷺ addressed the congregants by stating: "O people! You persisted on doing this until I thought that it was going to be prescribed for you." Then he ﷺ said:

فَصَلُّوا أَيُّهَا النَّاسُ فِي بُيُوتِكُمْ، فَإِنَّ أَفْضَلَ الصَّلَاةِ صَلَاةُ المَرْءِ
فِي بَيْتِهِ إِلَّا المَكْتُوبَةِ

"So offer your prayers in your houses, since a man's prayer is better in his house, except for the prescribed prayers."

But if you were blessed enough to pray behind him in the voluntary prayers, you would actually paradoxically regret it. Ibn Masʿūd ﷺ, who is the same person who learnt many surahs directly from the Prophet, said: "Once I saw the Prophet ﷺ performing the late-night prayers, so I joined him." This is supposed to be read as something amazing. Yet Ibn Masʿūd then said:

هَمَمْتُ بِأَمْرِ سُوءٍ

"But then I thought of doing something wrong."

They asked him: "What was that?" He said: "I thought of actually leaving the Prophet ﷺ mid-way in the prayer, while he was prostrating." Ḥudhayfah ibn al-Yamān ؓ also has a famous story along similar lines. He said that he once noticed the Prophet ﷺ performing the late-night prayers, so he decided to join him. He realised that the Prophet ﷺ was reading *Surah al-Baqarah* for the first *rak'ah*. He thought that the Prophet ﷺ would read only the first 100 verses, but the Prophet ﷺ continued. He then thought the Prophet ﷺ would read the first 200 verses, but the Prophet ﷺ continued reciting from the chapter. Then he thought that the Prophet ﷺ would bow after finishing *al-Baqarah* in its entirety. Much to his surprise, the Prophet ﷺ continued his recitation and began *Surah al-Nisā'*. Ḥudhayfah once again believed that the Prophet ﷺ would only recite portions of the chapter, but the Prophet also finished this chapter. Then the Prophet ﷺ proceeded to recite *Surah Āl 'Imrān*, and he finished all of it as well. Afterwards the Prophet ﷺ moved to the bowing position (*rukū'*). As Ḥudhayfah notes, the duration of the Prophet's bowing was as long as the time he spent standing. And he noted that the duration of every prostration (*sajdah*) was as long as the time he spent while bowing. In the second *rak'ah*, he ﷺ continued to read *al-Mā'idah*, *al-An'ām*, and other long chapters. Similarly, Umm Salamah ؓ notes in a fascinating narration that the Prophet ﷺ read the Seven Long Chapters (*al-sab' al-ṭiwāl*) in just one *rak'ah*.

The upshot of this presentation is that while his obligatory prayers were beautiful and delightful, he ﷺ kept them short. But if you had the opportunity to pray the late-night voluntary prayers with the Messenger ﷺ, you would have noticed how intensely connected he was with his Lord. He ﷺ would fully take his time by delivering the beautiful recitation that we all long to hear.

5

Sitting in His Circle

You have now had the opportunity to see the Prophet ﷺ during the Friday prayer and have had the chance to pray behind him. But now, you want to have the golden opportunity to sit in a gathering with him and observe his character and conduct. The young Companions enjoyed the morning sessions that they would convene with the Prophet ﷺ. The Prophet ﷺ would lead the Companions for the early Fajr prayer, and then afterwards sit in the *masjid* and remember Allah. This period of reflection would continue until the time of the Ḍuḥā prayer, which is done during the forenoon. He would be in a state of remembrance until sunrise, and in some cases he would continue this spiritual state of contemplation for longer.

Despite all his worship during the night, and even more worship after the morning, the Prophet ﷺ

would continue performing prayers after sunrise
as well. In fact, for the Ḍuḥā prayer, he would not
always just perform two *ra'kahs*, but instead he would
alternate between performing two, four, six or even
more *ra'kahs* after sunrise. And if he missed any
portion of his night (*qiyām*) prayers, he would make
them up between the Fajr and Ẓuhr prayers.

The Companions would also customarily sit in the
masjid and remember Allah during the morning;
they would patiently wait for the Prophet to finish
his Ḍuḥā prayer. The Messenger of Allah ﷺ was so
close to the youth that he would sit with any gathering
that he spotted in the *masjid*. ʿAlī ibn Abī Ṭālib ﷺ
described this practice of the Prophet ﷺ by stating:
"He would take whatever seat was available, and would
encourage others to do the same." Furthermore, when
the Prophet ﷺ sat in a gathering, he would give every
sitting companion of the assembly their rightful due
by giving them an equal amount of attention. By doing
this, every member of the gathering would feel equally
honoured. This means that he ﷺ would look at every
member, and interact with each one of them. That
way, no member of the congregation would feel that
they were of lesser importance than anyone else. Anas
ibn Mālik ﷺ, of course, was a young man. He said:
"No one was more beloved to us than the Messenger of
Allah ﷺ. However, if we saw him, we would not stand

*W*hen the Prophet ﷺ sat in a gathering, he would give every sitting companion an equal amount of attention so that every member would feel equally honoured. He ﷺ would look at every person, and interact with each one of them so that no one would feel that they were of lesser importance than others.

up for him because we knew how much he disliked that." He ﷺ was so humble that he would simply enter like anyone else; he did not like any special reception. And if anyone wanted to stand, he ﷺ would signal to them to sit down. He ﷺ would sit wherever a spot was open rather than going and assuming a place in the front. This practice of his was quite surprising, if not outright shocking. ʿAdī ibn Ḥātim al-Ṭāʾī ؓ says: "I came to the Prophet ﷺ to ask him about Islam, and the Prophet invited me to sit down. He then asked for a pillow, and he put it between us; he then put his arm on it. He then told me to put my own elbow on it as well. At that point I knew that this is not a king." He realised at that point that the Prophet ﷺ was not like the customary heads of state that existed at the time. ʿAlī ؓ also said: "If someone asked the Prophet ﷺ for something he needed, he would not send him away without what he had requested. At the very least, he would provide some words of comfort."

Jābir ibn Samurah ؓ was asked, "Did you used to sit with the Messenger of Allah ﷺ?" He said: "Yes. When the Prophet prayed Fajr, he would stay in his specific place, remembering Allah. But then he would come and join his Companions." What is fascinating is that Jābir ؓ mentioned that the Companions would discuss matters pertaining to the past Days of Ignorance (*jāhiliyyah*), recite words of poetry, and laugh.

During their discussions, the Prophet ﷺ would smile with them. It was the norm of the Prophet ﷺ to be silent, engage in the remembrance of Allah (*dhikr*), smile towards the people, and not dominate the discussion. He would also regularly make *istighfār* during these sessions, seeking Allah's forgiveness at least 70 times for every session. There was once a man who recited up to 100 lines from the poetry of Umayyah ibn Abī al-Ṣalt, and the Prophet ﷺ allowed him to freely do so. These facts and historical accounts might be surprising, but they show the beautiful nature of the Prophet ﷺ and his Companions. Ibn Sīrīn ﷺ was once asked whether the Companions of the Prophet ever had moments of joy and laughter amongst themselves. He responded by stating:

مَا كَانُوا إِلَّا كَالنَّاسِ، كَانَ ابْنُ عُمَرَ يَمْزَحُ وَيُنْشِدُ الشِّعْرَ

"They were not but people. Even Ibn ʿUmar used to joke and compose lines of poetry."

So these circles (*ḥalaqāt*) were not strictly about dedicating oneself to the remembrance of Allah. But it should be noted that the Prophet ﷺ never sat in a gathering or session which totally lacked the remembrance of Allah, or contained anything sinful or objectionable.

We find that some of the young Companions loved having the Prophet 爨 engage and participate in their discussions. Zayd ibn Thābit ﷺ said of his gatherings with the Prophet 爨:

إِذَا ذَكَرْنَا الدُّنْيَا ذَكَرَهَا مَعَنَا، وَإِذَا ذَكَرْنَا الآخِرَةَ ذَكَرَهَا مَعَنَا،
وَإِذَا ذَكَرْنَا الطَّعَامَ ذَكَرَهُ مَعَنَا

"When we spoke of worldly matters, he discussed them with us. When we spoke about the Hereafter (ākhirah), he spoke about it as well. And when we discussed issues pertaining to food, he engaged in discussion regarding them as well."

But when discussing worldly matters, the Prophet 爨 would only bring up matters of benefit. For instance, with regards to food, he 爨 would not bring up frivolous topics, but instead would point out beneficial regimens that people should have, the types of food they should try, and the different dishes he enjoyed. One of the famous hadiths regarding the Prophet's engagement with the youth is narrated by Ibn Masʿūd ﷺ. This Companion mentioned that they were once sitting in a gathering and discussing how they wanted to get married. As you can see, the Companions discussed topics pertaining to this world (*dunyā*) as well in the *masjid*, and did not only speak of matters pertaining to the Hereafter. The Prophet 爨 said to them:

يَا مَعْشَرَ الشَّبَابِ، مَنِ اسْتَطَاعَ مِنْكُمُ الْبَاءَةَ فَلْيَتَزَوَّجْ

"O young men! Whoever amongst you can afford to get married, let them do so. And whoever cannot, let them fast instead, and that will be a shield for them."

During these gatherings, the Prophet ﷺ would ask the Companions if they had seen any dreams the preceding night which they would like to share. He was of course referring to good dreams only, as he mentioned in other hadiths that bad dreams should not be narrated; instead, the person afflicted with one should seek refuge of Allah, and they will ultimately not be harmed. Every Companion wanted to see a good dream, so they could share it with the Prophet ﷺ and speak with him. In fact, ʿAbdullāh ibn ʿUmar ﷺ said: "I even made *duʿā'* to Allah by saying: 'O Allah! If You know of any good in me, then let me see a good dream so that I may share it with the Prophet ﷺ.'" He wanted this to happen, so he could have a conversation with the Prophet. Instead, Ibn ʿUmar saw a frightening dream, but the Prophet ﷺ still had it interpreted via Ibn ʿUmar's sister, Ḥafṣah ﷺ. So the Prophet ﷺ was the person that everyone in the gathering wanted to speak and communicate with. He was always approachable, sat in the gathering like everyone else, and maintained a tranquil position which did not affect the flow of the group conversations. Everyone was constantly

The Prophet ﷺ was always approachable, sat in the gathering like everyone else, and maintained a tranquil position which did not affect the flow of the group conversation. Everyone was constantly mindful of his presence, and wanted him to speak. Yet, he wanted the discussions to be fully inclusive during the sessions.

mindful of his presence, and wanted him to speak. Yet, during these small morning sessions, the Prophet ﷺ wanted the discussions to be fully inclusive. You can imagine the blessed Prophet sitting cross-legged during these sessions, while reclining on a cushion. He presented himself in his most basic and human form, yet his presence was always blessed.

The problem was that the women felt removed from these discussions. Abū Sa'īd ﷺ narrates that the women approached the Prophet ﷺ and said: "O Messenger of Allah! You hold gatherings with male Companions, but we get no chance to benefit from you." So the Prophet ﷺ said: "Gather together in this certain place and time, and I will come to you." He appointed a day of the week where they would hold a circle, and the Prophet ﷺ would come and provide advice and knowledge. In fact, the very first circle the Prophet ﷺ had with the women is where he shared with them the hadith: "Whoever amongst you loses three children, they will be a shield for you on the Day of Judgement." They said: "O Messenger of Allah, what about two?" He responded: "Even two."

While sitting with these different groups, the Prophet ﷺ always shared with them points of benefit and knowledge. He always ensured that by the conclusion of each session, every Companion had derived a benefit or was determined to perform an act containing a greater reward.

6

With Him in the Trenches

There is a noteworthy aphorism which states:

سَيِّدُ القَوْم خَادِمُهُمْ

"The leader of the people is their servant."

When the Prophet ﷺ came to Madinah, the residents of the city did not know what to expect from him. This is because the concept of servant leadership was foreign to them. Even in contemporary times, it is rare to find political leaders who genuinely serve the people, except in rare circumstances. Even then, such actions are often carried out for ulterior reasons. As for the Prophet ﷺ, he was so committed to serving his people that he had to be advised to not overburden himself. Yet every time this happened, he ﷺ still continued to serve the people. By doing so, he ﷺ taught them and us a lesson by showing us a vivid contrast to the typical pompous leadership that people have become accustomed to.

The Prophet ﷺ set the tone from the very beginning. He ﷺ came to Qubā' in Madinah, where the people were expecting to host and honour him in a way which befitted his eminent status. Their expectation was that the people would serve him, while the Prophet ﷺ would sit and lead. But the Prophet ﷺ entered Qubā' in such a discreet and humble manner that they could not even distinguish him from Abū Bakr ﷺ.

Furthermore, when they were building the first *masjid* of Islam, which is known as *Masjid* Qubā', the Prophet ﷺ played an active role in its building process. Likewise, when they conducted the construction process of the Prophet's *masjid* in Madinah, the Prophet ﷺ would carry the bricks himself and toil just like the rest of the workers. He worked as hard as the rest of the builders, by carrying the bricks and participating in every step of the construction operations.

Furthermore, he ﷺ would make *du'ā'* for the builders by saying:

اللَّهُمَّ إِنَّ الأَجْرَ أَجْرُ الآخِرَةِ فَارْحَمِ الأَنْصَارَ وَالْمُهَاجِرَةَ

"O Allah! Surely the true reward is that of the Hereafter. So have mercy upon the Helpers and the Emigrants."

So the Prophet ﷺ set a decisive tone early on after migrating to Madinah. If you lived in his society and time, you would have noticed that every year there was some form of conflict or hardship that afflicted the city. The Prophet ﷺ never found any time to rest, as Madinah—with its beauty and splendour—almost always found itself under attack or the threat of war. The question then is: what was it like to live with the Prophet ﷺ under the threat of war or violence? What was it like to live through the battles and conflicts the Prophet ﷺ and his community of believers had to face? We usually only read about these battles in books, but we should ask how we would find and view the Prophet ﷺ during these engagements? How would you view such circumstances, keeping in mind that one would have to be used to such threats on a regular basis?

In times of difficulty and war, the Messenger of Allah ﷺ never suffered less than his Companions. In the Battle of the Trench (*al-khandaq*), the Prophet ﷺ found himself in the defensive front and held the line. In fact, in preparation for the war, the Prophet ﷺ dug the share of ten men all by himself. Abū Ṭalḥah ﷺ narrates: "We showed the Prophet ﷺ the stones on our stomachs, which we used to alleviate our hunger. The Prophet ﷺ lifted up his own upper garment, and revealed that he had two stones on his stomach."

During the construction process of the Prophet's masjid in Madinah, the Prophet ﷺ would carry the bricks himself and toil just like the rest of the workers. He ﷺ worked as hard as the rest of the builders, by carrying the bricks and participating in every step of the construction operations.

This indicates that he ate even less than all his starving Companions, even though he was their leader.

They found themselves under a serious threat of invasion, and were committed to digging the defensive trenches as fast as possible. For this period, al-Barā' ﷺ narrates a moving hadith which indicates the Prophet's resilience and fortitude. It is probably one of my favourite narrations of the Prophet ﷺ and how he appeared. Al-Barā' ﷺ mentioned that the Prophet rose up on that day of battle, where he was completely covered with dirt. Dirt saturated every segment of his blessed skin. He ﷺ was there on the battle front, digging with them, striving to meticulously prepare the defensive capabilities, and suffering the same pains and struggles. He ﷺ looked at the soldiers and made *du'ā'* for them by saying:

اللَّهُمَّ لَا عَيْشَ إِلَّا عَيْشَ الآخِرَةِ فَارْحَم الأَنْصَارَ وَالمُهَاجِرَةَ

"O Allah! There is no life except for the life of the Hereafter. So have mercy on the Helpers and Emigrants."

So the Prophet ﷺ was constantly there in the front line, praying, chanting, and being supportive of his Companions.

Now, what was it like to go to battle with him? The night before a military contest, the Prophet 🌸 would spend the whole night in prayer, asking Allah for victory. To prepare himself for battle, he 🌸 had two metal suits of armour he would wear, and a sword, whose handle was made of silver. He had a black turban, but on some occasions he would wear a silver helmet. The Prophet 🌸 would preside before his army and directly address them with clear instructions. Before speaking of anything related to the battle tactics, he 🌸 would first always give instructions pertaining to the ethics and right conduct of war. He 🌸 would remind the Companions to not kill children, women, the elderly, or the sick. Furthermore, he 🌸 would forbid the Companions from practising treachery, mutilating anyone, harming monks and places of worship, or destroying trees or crops. Then the Prophet 🌸 would say: "Here is Jibrīl, and the angels ready to proceed." After these points and instructions, they would commence the battle.

In the battlefield the Prophet 🌸 was always ahead of everyone else. Despite his immense strength and courage, it is amazing to find ʿAlī ibn Abī Ṭālib 🌸 stating the following: "When the fighting intensified and the two sides met in battle, we sought shelter with the Messenger of Allah. No one was closer to the enemy than him." He 🌸 would always charge

The Prophet ﷺ was constantly there in the front line, praying, chanting, and being supportive of his Companions. He ﷺ was digging with them, striving to meticulously prepare the defensive capabilities, and suffering the same pains and struggles with his people.

forth, and never retreated from the battlefield. On this issue, we often talk about the Battle of Uḥud, where the Prophet ﷺ was wounded, yet he ﷺ still was able to keep the line. However, the Prophet's valiant efforts in the Battle of Ḥunayn were even more spectacular, as he ﷺ was only one amongst six people who remained in the battlefield. He ﷺ never turned back, even though he was on a mule. On the Battle of Ḥunayn, he ﷺ continued to charge forward, saying:

أَنَا النَّبِيُّ لَا كَذِبْ أَنَا ابْنُ عَبْدِ المُطَّلِبِ

"I am the Prophet, without any doubt. And I am the son of ʿAbd al-Muṭṭalib, with no doubt."

He ﷺ would charge forward without any fear, and would fight harder than anyone else. Yet what is even more amazing about him is that he ﷺ would always strive to merely disarm the enemy, and did not wish to kill any combatants. For all his military combats, he ﷺ only killed one person, and that was Ubayy ibn Khalaf during the Battle of Uḥud. Ubayy tried to charge at the Prophet ﷺ, but before he successfully reached him, the Prophet ﷺ threw a spear towards him and had him killed. Despite his great courage and strength, he ﷺ never sought to kill the enemy in the battlefield. ʿAlī ﷺ said that the Prophet ﷺ never struck anyone with his hand except while fighting in

the battlefield for the sake of Allah (*fī sabīlillāh*).
He ﷺ never struck a woman or a slave.

In addition to his courage, the Prophet ﷺ was known
for his mercy and concern for his fellow combatants
in the battlefield. After a military conflict finished, the
Prophet ﷺ would check up on all his Companions and
verify their state and condition. He ﷺ would pray for the
deceased himself, and console all their family members.

There is a beautiful narration which illustrates the
Prophet's unlimited courage. During the night an
alarming noise was heard right outside the city of
Madinah, and the inhabitants of the city feared
that they were being ambushed. The people quickly
militarised themselves and prepared for a potential
counter-attack, if it was found to be necessary. By the
time they mobilised themselves and planned to depart,
they found the Prophet ﷺ riding an unsaddled horse
and returning from the outskirts of Madinah. He ﷺ had
his sword hanging around his neck, and he told them:

لَا تَخَافُوا

"Do not be scared."

He ﷺ verified the source of the sound and found that
there was no active threat. This is the Messenger of

Allah ﷺ! If you were afraid in Madinah due to an event, he ﷺ would go out and make sure that everything was safe. He ﷺ would endure the most difficulty for the sake of Allah and for the ease of the people.

Celebrating With Him

Celebrations are meant to be simple and expansive. Unfortunately in our times we act contrary to these prescriptions, as we organise our celebrations in an extravagant and exclusive manner. This current practice is in fact the direct opposite of how the Prophet ﷺ used to have celebrations arranged during his lifetime.

We already explored how it was like to see the Messenger of Allah ﷺ during times of war and hardship. Likewise, we discussed how it was to spend the month of Ramadan in prayer and worship with the Prophet ﷺ. Now, however, I want to analyse the feasts, celebrations, and festivities that took place with the Prophet ﷺ. For a topic like this, it is most appropriate to start with the festival of Eid. During this discussion, I want to maintain the religious energy found in "Ramadan mode" while analysing the topic of Eid.

The Prophet ﷺ would foster a strong feeling of communal solidarity between Muslims on the day of Eid. He ﷺ would come out on this blessed and cheerful day wearing a beautiful red-striped Yemeni dress. He ﷺ appeared most pleasing with this exceptional attire, which he addressed the people with. He ﷺ would call the entire community to attend the service by saying: "Everyone come out to the Eid prayer." He would ensure that everyone came out and appeared at the prayer area: the men, the women, the elderly, and the children. The Prophet ﷺ ensured that he greeted every single person on this special occasion. Furthermore, he ﷺ would deliver his sermon (*khuṭbah*) differently on that day, as he stood closer to the people. He ﷺ would walk around with his Companions, and remind them of upholding Allah's commandments. We often perceive the day of Eid as being a time of heedlessness (*ghaflah*) rather than being a day of glorifying Allah and expressing gratitude to Him. The Prophet ﷺ would stress this dimension of worship and service to Him by repeating at the end of his sermon:

تَصَدَّقُوا تَصَدَّقُوا تَصَدَّقُوا

"Give charity, give charity, give charity."

So Eid was considered to be a day of charity in the time of the Prophet ﷺ. This was done in order to remind everyone to be grateful of their blessings, and ensure that the day was inclusive and allowed everyone to partake in the joys of the occasion. This is precisely the reason for why we have the legal obligation of *zakāt al-fiṭr* for Eid al-Fiṭr. This is so that everyone will be able to eat and feast on that day. Had this form of charity not existed, only the rich and well-to-do would enjoy the festivities. Likewise, Eid al-Aḍḥā is when the major sacrifice is made, which once again allows the poor to eat and be cheerful during the celebrations. Ultimately, on these days the Prophet ﷺ reminded people to be generous, open and friendly to others, and remember Allah. Sometimes it was difficult to discern the boundaries of the degree of openness allowed, so the Prophet ﷺ defined those limits. There is an important narration which states that on Eid two young girls were singing songs about the Battle of Buʿāth, which occurred during pre-Islamic times. Abū Bakr ﷺ harshly reprimanded those girls, and ordered them to stop singing in the Prophet's presence. However, the Prophet ﷺ stopped Abū Bakr by stating: "Leave them. Every people has a day of Eid, and this is our Eid." He allowed them to continue singing, as they were not saying anything objectionable.

'Ā'ishah 鬱 likewise describes how she spent the day of
Eid with the Prophet in a special way. She mentioned
how the Prophet was lying down. When Abū Bakr 鬱
left, she asked the Prophet if they could go and watch
the Abyssinians, who were performing their special
war dances in the *masjid*. These were dances which
they performed with their spears and shields; their
movements did not contain anything objectionable.
The Prophet 鬱 concurred and took 'Ā'ishah 鬱
with him. The Prophet sat in front of 'Ā'ishah 鬱;
'Ā'ishah put her head on his shoulder behind him,
such that her cheek touched his. He approved of
the Abyssinians' warrior dance, and told them to
carry on. They thus continued performing their war
exercise. After watching them for a moment, the
Prophet 鬱 asked 'Ā'ishah:

حَسْبُكِ؟

"Have you had enough?"

She said no, as she wanted to see if the Prophet 鬱
would be patient with her and further allow her to see
the celebrations. After the passage of some time, she
started to get tired from standing and watching. The
Prophet 鬱 asked her if she was satisfied. She once again
replied in the negative. After standing and watching
them for a further duration of time, she told the
Prophet 鬱 that she had enough. The Prophet 鬱 then

*O*n the day of Eid,
the Prophet ﷺ was
immensely generous.
He ﷺ was determined to
serve the people and give
them the necessary means
so they could celebrate.
He ensured that he could
celebrate the special day
with everyone.

took her home after they witnessed the celebrations. The Prophet's presence and lack of disapproval of the dances of these Abyssinians means that such forms of celebration are permissible.

We also know that in respect to the Eid prayer, the Prophet ﷺ would take one route to go to the place of prayer, and would trek another path when returning back home. The rationale for why he ﷺ did so relates to motives based on spirituality (*tazkiyah*), as the use of a different route back home symbolises that one is adopting a new path in their life. Another explanation which the scholars have provided for this consistent prophetic practice is that by taking two paths the Prophet ﷺ could issue his greeting (*salām*) to the inhabitants of the opposing sides (*ahl al-ṭarīqayn*) of the neighbourhoods, regardless of which path they lived in. Likewise, by doing this, the Prophet ﷺ could encounter and identify anyone who had financial needs, and then give them charity (*ṣadaqah*). This was a day where the Prophet ﷺ was immensely generous, and he ﷺ was determined to serve the people and give them the necessary means so they could celebrate. He ﷺ served the people, and ensured that he could celebrate the special day with everyone. Because he ﷺ took a different path home, everyone living in the city of Madinah could celebrate Eid with him.

As for the case of weddings, the Prophet ﷺ
would encourage people to have banquets, but he
discouraged any form of extravagance. Sometimes
only simple dishes of meat and bread would be served.
In a number of cases, only bread was available. In
other scenarios, a few dates, milk, and clarified
butter were available. On another set of occasions
ḥays was served, which was one of the Prophet's
favourite dishes. This dish consists of a mixture of
date paste, clarified fat, and yogurt. Sometimes only
barley was available. But in any case, the Prophet ﷺ
ate anything that was there, and would celebrate with
the people. We even find that for such occasions the
Prophet ﷺ would organise potlucks, where everyone
would prepare what they could and share their food
with others. This in fact was how he ﷺ prepared his
wedding with Ṣafiyyah ﷺ. This mode of arrangement
was simple but blessed: everyone brought whatever
food they had, and they ate together.

Black leather mats were brought and placed on the
ground, so people from all over the city could attend,
eat, and join in the festivities. Regarding banquets
and similar gatherings where food is served, the
Prophet ﷺ expressed to us a very serious warning
when he said: "The worst feast is the one to which
only the rich are invited and the poor are excluded."

If you want your banquet or special occasion to have blessings (*barakah*), do not exclude the poor. Do not make your event exclusively small such that only the rich are invited. Instead, make it simple, inclusive, and open to the poor as well. The latter was the consistent habit of the Prophet ﷺ and what he prescribed for his *ummah*.

Likewise, the Prophet ﷺ would attend all the weddings that he could, and would not simply restrict himself to celebrating the events of the upper elite. Furthermore, when a poor person was getting married, the Prophet ﷺ would encourage everyone to contribute to this person's wedding expenses, and he would even help finance their allotted dowry amounts. Even when ʿAlī ﷺ married the Prophet's daughter Fāṭimah ﷺ, all members of the Prophet's household participated in that wedding by preparing food and undertaking the rest of the arrangements. The Prophet ﷺ himself furnished the house of ʿAlī ﷺ. When the Prophet ﷺ participated in celebrations, he did not just shower the gathering with blessings, but he also changed paradigms. He ﷺ ensured that all celebrations were community-centred, whereby no-one was left out.

When He Played With Your Kids

If you recall your childhood memories, you might remember many of the adults—whether they were relatives or not—who were kind with you. You might recall how some of them told you funny jokes, while others were very playful with you. Children can detect these types of welcoming mannerisms, as they can very easily discern gestures of kindness or crassness. This is the reason why the Prophet ﷺ said:

لَيْسَ مِنَّا مَنْ لَمْ يَرْحَمْ صَغِيرَنَا، وَيُوَقِّرْ كَبِيرَنَا

"The one who fails to show mercy to the young ones is not among us, nor the one who does not uphold respect for the elderly."

Anas ibn Mālik ؓ said: "I never saw anyone more merciful with children than the Prophet ﷺ." When someone brought their child in the presence of the

Prophet ✹, he would do anything but ignore it. He would actively play and converse with them. This type of affection naturally caused these children to develop a strong connection with the Prophet ✹, and by extension, allowed them to develop an affinity with the *masjid*. If the *masjid* has a kind and caring imam, the child will definitely want to see them on a regular basis. The children of the Companions enjoyed going to the *masjid*, since they knew that the Prophet ✹ was going to converse, play with them, and even give them gifts. The friendly culture which the Prophet ✹ fostered meant that the children loved to be around him. Anas ✸ said: "The Prophet ✹ used to mix with us so much that he would ask one of my little brothers named Abū ʿUmayr about his bird—known as *Nughayr*—by saying:

يَا أَبَا عُمَيْرٍ، مَا فَعَلَ النُّغَيْرِ

'O Abū ʿUmayr! What happened with Nughayr?'"

So every time Anas's brother passed by him, the Prophet ✹ asked him about his pet bird, and would take interest in it. By asking children about their interests and activities, the Prophet ✹ developed strong relationships with them. Those children would eventually grow up to become prominent scholars of this *ummah*. They were young junior Companions, but they had the opportunity to interact with the

Prophet ﷺ and learn knowledge from the senior Companions. These junior Companions were instrumental in providing vital religious training to the next generation, known as the Successors (Tābiʿūn).

How did this relationship between the Prophet ﷺ and children start? It actually began with the birth of the child. It was customary for the Companions to bring their newborn baby immediately to the Prophet ﷺ, so that he could name, bless, and perform *duʿā'* over them. Of course, the greatest thing which the Prophet ﷺ did for the newborn was to perform the *taḥnīk* process, where he would rub a chewed date against the palate of the newborn. This is something that the Companions always requested from the Prophet ﷺ, and he would oblige. Anas ﷺ mentions that when ʿAbdullāh ﷺ the son of Abū Ṭalḥah ﷺ was born, the Prophet ﷺ held him in his lap, put a date in his own mouth, and then rubbed it against ʿAbdullāh's palate. ʿAbdullāh ﷺ really enjoyed the taste of that date. This is why the Prophet ﷺ said:

حُبُّ الأَنْصَارِ التَّمْرُ

"This is how the Helpers are; they love dates."

And he named him ʿAbdullāh. A lot of the children of the Companions were in fact named by the Prophet ﷺ.

Children would grab the Prophet ﷺ by the hand, show him things that interested them, and would try to play games alongside him. He ﷺ would never turn away from them or leave them until they were fully satisfied.

Whenever he came across Abyssinian children, the Prophet ﷺ would try to converse with them in their own language. He ﷺ would often stumble while trying to speak their native tongue. Sometimes he ﷺ would do that on purpose so they would laugh with him. Children would grab him by the hand, show him things that interested them, and would try to play games alongside him. The Messenger of Allah ﷺ would never turn away from them or leave them until they were fully satisfied.

There are beautiful narrations which highlight how the Prophet ﷺ would give the youth precedence over himself. During Madinah's harvest season, it was customary for the farmers of the city to provide some of their fresh produce to the Prophet ﷺ, so he may bless their crops and make *du'ā'* for them as well. It was the Prophet's custom to always give the fruits he received to a nearby child belonging to his *ummah*, by calling them over and handing them the produce. Even though the farmers desired that the Prophet ﷺ consume the fruit, the Prophet would prefer to give it to a child. This was in many respects similar to giving candy, but a much healthier and blessed form of it.

The Prophet's relationship with his grandchildren was a sight of utmost beauty. With regards to al-Ḥusayn and al-Ḥasan ﷺ, the Prophet did not just express his

love to them through his actions by holding them
and articulating his affection towards them, but he
would loudly invoke Allah by saying: "O Allah, love
those who love them." He would hold them with deep
affection and kiss them.

Fāṭimah ✿ mentions that whenever the Prophet used
to visit her house, he would state:

أَثَمَّ لُكَعُ؟ أَثَمَّ لُكَعُ؟

"Where is the little one? Where is the little one?"

By posing this question he was referring to al-Ḥasan.
He would often request that all his grandchildren
and young loved ones be brought before him, and he
would gather all of them together under his cloak:
al-Ḥasan, al-Ḥusayn, Zaynab, Umāmah, and Usāmah
ibn Zayd. He would hold them close to himself and
make *duʿā'* for each one of them. The Prophet's actions
changed paradigms and transformed the culture of
the city of Madinah. A man once saw the Prophet ﷺ
kissing, hugging, and playing with al-Ḥusayn and
al-Ḥasan ✿. He remarked that he had ten children,
yet he never gave them affection, as that is not the
normal behaviour of men. In response, the Prophet ﷺ
said: "What can I do about a man who has no mercy?
Whoever does not show mercy will not have mercy
shown to them." The Prophet ﷺ thus emphasised

that it is absolutely imperative that we display love, affection, and mercy (*raḥmah*) to our children.

The Prophet ﷺ would exert additional efforts to display love and affection to orphans, since they were often deprived of parental connections. The Prophet ﷺ knew that they needed this attention, since he himself grew up as an orphan. He ﷺ said: "The best house is the one in which orphans are treated well. The worst house is the one in which orphans are treated poorly." Just like how he ﷺ criticised exclusive feasts which excluded the poor, he likewise censured the houses which failed to treat the orphans well.

He ﷺ always tried to give orphans emotional support, and ensured that they formed connections with an adult figure like himself. This is why he ﷺ told Abū al-Dardā' ﷺ that if he wanted to have his heart softened and have his provisions fulfilled in life, he should do the following:

أَدْنِ الْيَتِيمَ مِنكَ، وَأَلْطِفْهُ، وَامْسَحْ بِرَأْسِهِ، وَأَطْعِمْهُ مِن طَعَامِكَ؛ فَإِنَّ ذَلِكَ يُلَيِّنُ قَلْبَكَ، وَيُدْرِكُ حَاجَتَكَ

"Bring the orphan near to you, caress his hair, and feed him from the food that you eat. That will soften your heart and fulfill your needs."

The Prophet ﷺ himself would do this; he would invite orphans (*aytām*) to his house and walk with them. Because they were subject to exploitation and abuse, he ﷺ would defend them and intercede on their behalf for any difficulties they may have faced. While the Prophet ﷺ cared and loved children of the *ummah* as a whole, he ensured to pay special attention to these vulnerable children, who lacked parental support and adult guidance.

Inviting Him to Your Home

You have been able to see the Prophet ﷺ from afar. You have had the chance to listen to his sermon for the Friday prayer. You have also had the chance to pray behind him. You have seen and interacted with him in times of difficulty, such as battles. You have likewise had the opportunity to see him in the context of celebrations, feasts, and the days of Eid. You even had the opportunity to attend some small gatherings with him. But now, you want to take things a step further and actually invite the Prophet ﷺ to your house. What should you know before you approach the Prophet ﷺ and say: "O Messenger of Allah (*Yā Rasūlallāh*), will you please come to my house?"

First and foremost, one should know that the Prophet ﷺ said: "I will accept the invitation of anyone, even if all they have to serve me is the arm or foot of a sheep."

So you would never have to consider scarcity of food as being a negative factor. Regardless of how little you had to serve, the Prophet ﷺ would still come. Furthermore, the Prophet ﷺ would not restrict himself to only accepting the invitations of the elite class. Anas ؆ said that the Messenger of Allah would visit the sick, attend funerals (*janā'iz*), ride donkeys, and accept invitations, even from those who were enslaved. It is amazing that slaves in Madinan society would invite the Prophet ﷺ, as this was something uncommon to hear; yet he would always accept their invitations. Through this narration, Anas ؆ was indicating the beautiful and open nature of the Prophet ﷺ. When visiting the sick, it did not concern him whether this was a powerful person or not. Likewise, he ﷺ attended and prayed for the funerals of all classes of people. Furthermore, he ﷺ even rode on the lowliest of animals. Lastly, he ﷺ accepted any invitation, no matter how humble it was.

Now, the Prophet ﷺ has accepted your invitation, and you are trying to prepare for his arrival. What should you serve him? We know that he did not like extravagant foods, but at the same time you do want to give him something that he enjoys. The Prophet ﷺ was known to like cold and sweet drinks, like milk, and water sweetened with honey. He lived in a desert climate, and it is evident that his preferences reflected that. In terms of food, the Prophet ﷺ was very simple insofar as he liked to eat bread spread or dipped in a condiment. He ﷺ would sometimes eat it with honey, which he loved. He ﷺ also sometimes ate it with *ḥays*, which was a mixture of date paste, yogurt, and fat. If you had only oil, he ﷺ would dip bread in it and eat it. Even if you just had vinegar, the Prophet ﷺ would enjoy eating bread with it. He ﷺ is recorded to have said: "What an excellent condiment vinegar is!" If you took some bread and rubbed it in vinegar, the Prophet ﷺ would accept it and eat it.

With regards to meat, the Prophet ﷺ enjoyed eating the shoulder of the lamb. On this matter, 'Ā'ishah ﷺ has a famous hadith where she told the Prophet ﷺ that she donated everything from a lamb except its shoulder. She ﷺ intentionally saved this portion because she knew how much the Prophet ﷺ loved it. After informing the Prophet ﷺ of this matter, he said in response: "Rather everything remains of it except the shoulder." What he ﷺ meant by this was that she did not attain any reward (*ajr*) for the shoulder, as she did not give it away as charity (*ṣadaqah*).

From among the eminent virtues and manners of the Prophet ﷺ is that he would never criticise food, nor would he overpraise it. The scholars mention the subtle wisdoms for why the Prophet ﷺ would never

overpraise food. It is because that if in a certain
scenario he did not excessively praise a dish, a person
would then think that something was perhaps wrong
with it. Instead, the Prophet ﷺ was always grateful
for any type of food that he received. Likewise, he ﷺ
never dismissed or criticised food; there is in fact no
narration which indicates that he did such a thing.
Instead, he ﷺ would always thank the server of food,
so that no high or unreasonable standards would be set.

But of course, if the Prophet ﷺ enjoyed a dish, it
would be obvious. The Prophet ﷺ had a Persian
neighbour who would always make a delicious broth,
and he used to send some of it to the Prophet ﷺ.
Because this neighbour knew of the Prophet's love for
this particular dish, he once approached the Prophet ﷺ
and invited him to his house to eat some of it with
him. The Prophet ﷺ pointed to his wife ʿĀʾishah ؓ
and asked:

وَهَذِهِ؟

"Can she come too?"

The neighbour refused. The Prophet ﷺ declined the
invitation. The next day the neighbour approached
the Prophet ﷺ and issued the same invitation. Once
again, the Prophet ﷺ asked if ʿĀʾishah could come,
and the neighbour once again refused. So the

The Prophet ﷺ was always grateful for any type of food that he received. There is no narration which indicates that he dismissed or criticised food. Instead, he ﷺ would always thank the server of food, so that no high or unreasonable standards would be set.

Prophet ﷺ declined to accept his invitation. The
neighbour then approached the Prophet ﷺ again for a
third time, giving the same invitation. The Prophet ﷺ
once again asked if he could bring ʿĀʾishah along with
him. This time the neighbour allowed her to come as
well. So the Prophet ﷺ accepted the invitation and
came with ʿĀʾishah.

Imam al-Nawawī ﷺ commented on this report by
noting that the Prophet ﷺ disliked to attend a special
event without being accompanied by ʿĀʾishah. This
was a very unique way of the Prophet ﷺ indicating
the high consideration he gave for his family. His
society had not learnt or become accustomed to such
values yet, but his acts were instrumental in bringing
about a serious paradigm shift.

When going to someone's house, the Prophet ﷺ would
often bring with him the Ahl al-Ṣuffah, that is, the
poor Companions who lived adjacent to his *masjid*.
Likewise, he ﷺ would bring with him orphans or
people who were hungry. These different groups
and strata were always his subject of concern—the
forgotten ones.

Would you not want him to come to your house,
make *duʿāʾ* for you, sit with you, and also thank you?
He ﷺ would do all these things when attending a

person's house. Of course, from this point on your relations with the Prophet ﷺ are likely to be stronger and more blessed. But perhaps the greatest virtue that the host derived was that the Prophet ﷺ would bless their house by praying in it. By doing so, the owners of the house would feel a special connection with that specific location and take it as a place of prayer (*muṣallā*). The Prophet ﷺ knew that the people valued this, and so he would pray in their homes. Regarding this matter, Anas ﷺ reported the following hadith:

صَلَّيْتُ أَنَا وَيَتِيمٌ فِي بَيْتِنَا خَلْفَ النَّبِيِّ صَلَّى اللهُ عَلَيْهِ وَسَلَّمَ، وَأُمِّي أُمُّ سُلَيْمٍ خَلْفَنَا

"[The Prophet ﷺ was a guest in our home and] I prayed behind the Prophet ﷺ, with an orphan standing beside me, while Umm Sulaym stood behind our row."

Umm Sulaym ﷺ was the mother of Anas ﷺ. Anas reports another hadith, but this time it was his grandmother named Mulaykah ﷺ who invited the Prophet ﷺ, as she wanted the Prophet ﷺ to eat from her food. After finishing the meal, the Prophet ﷺ requested that they perform a short prayer together. Anas then said: "So I brought out this one rug (*ḥaṣīr*) that we had, which was old and worn-out. We all prayed two *rakʿahs* on it together, and then the

Prophet ☙ left." All this meant that the Prophet ☙
would not just visit these houses to develop a stronger
spiritual connection with his hosts. He would also
ensure that he blessed your house through his *du'ā'*
and prayer. That way, the residents of the house
would always be connected with him, regardless of
whether he was physically present or not.

10

When He Joked With You

Joking is a double-edged sword. The way that you joke actually says a lot about you. It is something that we should really take seriously, in terms of the ethics that surround it. Sometimes jokes can fully humiliate someone, while in other cases they may actually increase someone in honour. In other circumstances, they can strip a person of their dignity, as they can reveal unpleasant facts about a person. In other cases, they can be an exceptional source of joy. This is all then to say that the ruling on a certain joke depends on your intention, how it is employed, and who you are joking with.

If you had the chance to hear the Prophet ﷺ joke for the first time, you probably would have been taken aback. After all, he is the Messenger of Allah ﷺ, and you hold him in high esteem. You would have

seen him always exercise his conduct in the most
honourable and dignified manner. So the first time
you hear a joke from him, you would be somewhat
surprised. In fact, this is what several of the Companions
actually experienced with the Prophet ※. After hearing
humorous remarks from the Prophet ※, they would
ask in surprise: "O Messenger of Allah! You joke with
us?" In response, the Prophet ※ said:

إِنِّي لَأَمْزَحُ وَلَا أَقُولُ إِلَّا حَقًّا

"I joke, but I only speak the truth when doing so."

This means that even while joking, the Prophet ※ lived
up to his honourable titles of *al-Ṣādiq* and *al-Amīn*,
which he was bestowed with even before starting
his religious mission. These titles were given to the
Prophet ※ to indicate his honesty and trustworthy
character. Ultimately, the Prophet ※ would not tell a
joke if it contained any lies or deception. To discourage
others from falling in this, he said:

أَنَا زَعِيمٌ بِبَيْتٍ فِي وَسَطِ الْجَنَّةِ لِمَنْ تَرَكَ الْكَذِبَ وَإِنْ كَانَ مَازِحًا

"I guarantee a house in the centre of Paradise for the
one who leaves off lying, even if they are joking."

When analysing the jokes of the Prophet ※, one should
not become upset if they do not find them to be funny.
This is because jokes usually do not translate very well

across different cultures and languages. You might not even find the jokes of your parents to be funny, and vice versa. This renders jokes to be context-specific. We must also take into account the fact that the Prophet ﷺ stated these jokes more than 1400 years ago, and they were mentioned in a specific place and setting. The original recipients of these statements would have found them to be funny, though that might not be the case in contemporary times.

But in any case, there is an inherent beauty to how the Prophet ﷺ used to joke. Much of his humour centred inside his own household. As ʿĀʾishah ﷺ mentioned, if a non-serious matter arose with his family, the Prophet ﷺ would try make a joke out of the situation. She also noted that the Prophet ﷺ was a great jester (*mazzāḥ*) inside his own home, always joking with his family. His ultimate purpose through these jokes was to bring joy inside the household, and to foster an amicable atmosphere. Fostering happiness was the goal which he sought to achieve through all his attributes. As for the jokes that he ﷺ said, they were always intelligent, truthful, appropriate, and had a certain goal in mind. They were always used in order to solidify the bonds with family, friends, orphans, youth, and other members of the wider community. The use of jokes is effective to remove any formalities and strict modes of conduct; the

The Prophet ﷺ prohibited people from making jokes that mocked others or jokes that frightened or shocked people. Instead, he ﷺ used humour as a means to raise the people in value and honour as well as defuse tensions and disputes.

Prophet ﷺ made proper use of them to relax anyone's sense of nervousness and enable them to form authentic relationships.

The Prophet ﷺ also used jokes as a means to defuse tensions and disputes. This is perhaps a reflection of his great genius. Once Fāṭimah ﷺ and ʿAlī ﷺ got into an argument with one another, which is something that normally happens between married couples. The Prophet went to Fāṭimah's house and asked where ʿAlī ﷺ was. She ﷺ replied by saying that he was upset and went to the *masjid*. The Prophet went to the *masjid*, where he found ʿAlī ﷺ sleeping on the dirt. The Prophet began to dust the dirt off him and said:

قُمْ يَا أَبَا تُرَابٍ

"Stand up, O Abū Turāb!"

Abū Turāb translates to "father of dust". He gave ʿAlī that name jokingly in order to defuse the situation and allow him to reconcile with his wife.

In other cases, the Prophet ﷺ would employ jokes in order to explain a complicated or sensitive concept. A person might have been nervous or confused by a given topic before, so the Prophet ﷺ would cite a joke to beautifully explain it. For example, the Prophet ﷺ once told an old woman that no aged person will enter Paradise. Upon hearing this, the woman was saddened and started to cry. The Prophet ﷺ then explained that nobody would enter Paradise as an old person; instead, Allah would make everyone enter it in a youthful form. He was able to explain this point to the woman in a creative and thoughtful manner, such that he relieved her of any anxiety.

The fourth purpose of his jokes was in order to provide the ignored and overlooked members of society attention. He would carry out conversations with the weak and lower strata of society by sharing with them jokes and light-hearted remarks. For example, there is an incredible and moving story of the Companion Zāhir ibn Ḥarām ﷺ, who was a young man that was fairly unattractive in his appearance, and did not belong to any tribe. He therefore lacked any friends or allies who conversed or developed a friendship with him. The Prophet ﷺ would try to lift Zāhir's status by pointing him out in gatherings and inflating his importance.

The Prophet ﷺ would try to lift his spirits and often made jokes with him. There is one beautiful story where the Prophet ﷺ grabbed Zāhir ﷺ from behind in the marketplace, and loudly shouted to everyone around him:

مَنْ يَشْتَرِي هَذَا العَبْدُ؟ مَنْ يَشْتَرِي هَذَا العَبْدُ؟ مَنْ يَشْتَرِي هَذَا العَبْدُ؟

"Who will buy this slave? Who will buy this slave?
Who will buy this slave?"

At first, Zāhir ﷺ did not know that it was the
Prophet ﷺ who was doing this, so he was at first
shocked. But he then realised that it was the Prophet
ﷺ, so he did not resist or say anything, as he wanted
to benefit from the blessing (*barakah*) of being so
close to him. He submitted himself to the Prophet's
playful move, who held Zāhir ﷺ and joked with
him throughout the process. Zāhir's self-esteem was
so low that he told the Prophet that even if he really
was a slave for sale, nobody would want to buy him.
However, the Prophet ﷺ turned Zāhir ﷺ towards
him and said to him in the eye:

وَلٰكِنَّكَ عِندَ اللهِ غَالٍ

"However, you are indeed priceless in the
sight of Allah."

He ﷺ thus raised his spirits with this statement,
and cheered him up. He ﷺ enjoyed making these
jokes with the downtrodden, as they helped provide
them attention, and allowed him to form intimate
relationships with them.

We must appreciate and understand how the Prophet ✿ set the rules surrounding joking and humour. He ✿ prohibited people from making jokes that mocked others. Likewise, he ✿ barred any jokes that would frighten or shock others, such as taking the wealth of people or causing people to fall into a state of panic. Instead, he ✿ used humour as a means to raise the people in value and honour, not humiliate them. By using jokes in this manner, he ✿ was building greater bonds, instead of offending people. Ultimately, this created a cohesive community with strong social solidarity, where everyone felt connected first and foremost with him.

11

When You Thought You Were His Best Friend

A t this point, you have had the opportunity of inviting the Prophet ﷺ to your own house. He ﷺ has had the chance to familiarise himself with your name and has even shared jokes with you. But even more so, the Prophet ﷺ had a unique skill of making you perceive yourself as being the most beloved person of the gathering. He ﷺ would do this, even though there were many others who were ranked above you in honour and nobility. That was undoubtedly from his mercy and love for his Companions.

'Alī ﷺ describes the Prophet ﷺ in an interesting manner in this regard. He stated that the people were always attracted to the Prophet ﷺ and wanted to be close to him. He ﷺ was the direct opposite of someone who turned people away from their faith or caused them to be repelled. Instead, he ﷺ functioned like a magnet, where everyone had an affinity towards him. If you saw the Prophet ﷺ, you would want to be around him and would naturally love Allah more in his presence. ʿAlī ؓ even noted that the Prophet ﷺ was observant of the different ranks and titles that people assumed, and ensured that they would continue to uphold them. At the same time, however, we have noted how the Prophet ﷺ would uplift the status of the lower and marginalised strata on the basis of their piety.

But then ʿAlī ؓ notes that the Prophet ﷺ would exercise a degree of wariness vis-à-vis the people. Yes, the Prophet ﷺ displayed his kind and blessed conduct and was always providing the other side a warm smile. Yet, he ﷺ exercised a degree of caution. He was not naive, and always maintained a degree of scrupulousness. Yes, he ﷺ showed the best manners (*akhlāq*) to everyone, but to be an effective and competent leader, he had to keep his guard at all times. This type of restraint did not lead him to mistreat or harm anyone, but it was a layer of security required in order to uphold the integrity of the community.

Because of his collegiality, impeccable character, and friendliness, you would have assumed that the Prophet ﷺ was your best friend. If one was to carefully scan the different hadith collections, they will find numerous cases where the Prophet ﷺ gave personal pieces of advice (*naṣīḥah*) to his Companions on an individual basis. It is likely the case that we might not have even known the names of these Companions had they not reported these hadiths pertaining to personal advice, which were addressed to the people. Likewise, we find numerous cases where the Prophet ﷺ addressed an individual and gave them sincere and applicable personal advice. These words of wisdom eventually found their way into the famous collections of hadith, such that we all may use them as standards to regulate our normative behaviour.

Throughout his life, the Prophet ﷺ was a guiding figure who loved to give personal advice and attention to the members of his *ummah*. He ﷺ also enjoyed exchanging gifts and presents with others. Al-Rubayyiʿ ﷺ once stated: "I brought the Prophet ﷺ a tray of dates and small cucumbers." She gave the Prophet cucumbers as she knew the Prophet ﷺ enjoyed their taste. She noted that in return, the Prophet ﷺ gave her a handful of jewellery. ʿĀʾishah ﷺ stated that whenever the Prophet ﷺ received gifts from someone, he would always give them a present in return. You can only imagine how many times the Prophet ﷺ received gifts and presents from his followers and friends. Nevertheless, on every occasion, the Prophet ﷺ

would make a mental note to give this person a gift in return immediately afterwards, or a later point in the future.

We have had the chance to see and evaluate the richness of the Prophet's conversations, as well as his thoughtful humour. Jarīr ﷺ said: "I never saw the Prophet ﷺ except that he was smiling towards me." We derive a subtle but important benefit from this hadith. It is not just that the Prophet ﷺ used to smile, but he ﷺ used to smile warmly towards his followers. In addition, we have now noted how he ﷺ used to exchange gifts with his beloved followers. We also have a very noteworthy hadith from the Companion ʿAmr ibn al-ʿĀṣ ﷺ, who was once a fierce opponent of the Prophet by waging war against him for numerous years. ʿAmr had even tried to convince the Negus (Najāshī) to deport all the Companions who had sought refuge in Abyssinia (Ḥabashah). In fact, in the Battle of Uḥud, ʿAmr was one of the great masterminds who plotted that great counter-attack at the end of the contest, which led to the death of many eminent Muslims. However, it was from the immense blessings of Allah that he later accepted Islam and became one of the beloved Companions of the Prophet ﷺ. The Prophet ﷺ treated him with so much respect and love that he thought that he was likely now one of the best friends of the Prophet ﷺ.

There were numerous individuals who felt worthless or miserable, but after interacting with the Prophet ﷺ and being blessed with his kind attention, they began to feel that they were the most valued and beloved of people in the sight of the Prophet ﷺ, as he was to them.

To illustrate the Prophet's kindness and openness, 'Amr narrates that the Prophet ﷺ would show love, attention, and affection to the worst of people (*asharr al-qawm*) to the extent that they would believe that they were the best of people (*ashraf al-qawm*). 'Amr explained that this was a systematic method of connecting hearts together (*ta'līf*), which the Prophet ﷺ employed to bring people to guidance, happiness, and salvation.

As a result of the attention that the Prophet ﷺ gave him, 'Amr ☀ began to think that he might be the Prophet's best friend and Companion. His beliefs became further reinforced once the Prophet ﷺ appointed him as a commander of an army division. So he once went to the Prophet ﷺ in the presence of the people, and said:

يَا رَسُولَ اللهِ أَيُّ النَّاسِ أَحَبُّ إِلَيْكَ

"O Messenger of Allah! Who is the most beloved to you among the people?"

You can imagine how amazing of a spectacle this was, as 'Amr ☀ posed this question in public, while earnestly waiting for an answer. The Prophet ﷺ did not lie, and he immediately gave his answer: "'Ā'ishah." But 'Amr ☀ immediately indicated that he was requesting to know who the Prophet ﷺ loved most among men, by stating:

مِنَ الرِّجَالِ

"From the men?"

For the men in the audience, the Prophet's first response was strange, as it was uncommon for someone to love their wife more than anyone else. This is just like how the Prophet's deep affection for his children was unorthodox within the setting of his society. In any case, after being asked which male he loved the most, he ﷺ said:

أَبُوهَا

"Her father."

This was a reference to Abū Bakr ﷺ. The Prophet ﷺ could have mentioned Abū Bakr by name, but instead he sought to connect his name with the immense love he had for ʿĀʾishah. This answer was clearly understandable from ʿAmr's point of view, as Abū Bakr was the first male to accept Islam and the best friend of the Prophet. ʿAmr continued his interrogation by asking who came next. The Prophet ﷺ said that the second male Companion who he loved the most was ʿUmar ﷺ. ʿAmr was disappointed to not hear his name be mentioned next, but he understood that both

Abū Bakr and ʿUmar ☙ were eminent Companions, as they held the title of the Two Shaykhs (*Shaykhān*). The Prophet ☙ would always set his name side by side with the names of these two senior Companions, whether it be in explaining his decisions or when mentioning who came after him in rank. ʿAmr ultimately had his hopes that he might be mentioned afterwards. He asked the Prophet ☙ who he loved next. The Prophet ☙ said: "ʿUthmān." ʿAmr ceased questioning the Prophet ☙ anymore regarding who followed, and he explained that decision by saying: "I became silent for fear that he might never mention my name."

Of course, it was not the Prophet's intention to make ʿAmr ☙ feel this way at the end. But it was in fact the Prophet ☙ who made ʿAmr ☙ feel special and confident to the extent that he felt that he could possibly be identified as being his most beloved friend. This fact in itself is remarkable. There were in fact numerous individuals who felt that they were worthless or miserable, but after interacting with the Prophet ☙ and being blessed with his kind attention, their perceptions radically changed. They began to feel that they were the most valued and beloved of people in the sight of the Prophet ☙, as he was to them.

12

When You Needed His Help

Imam Ibn Taymiyyah ﷺ once made the following remarkable statement: "Even your shadow leaves you in the dark." We often discover in our lives that during the circumstances where we have urgent needs, the individuals we thought we could rely upon for help turn out to be entirely absent. That void drives you to the remembrance of Allah ﷻ, where you turn to Him and call upon Him alone. Hopefully, such intense devotion to Allah ﷻ alone might inspire you to never forsake others. Instead, by seeking Allah's help, you may become inspired to be a supporter when others need your assistance. As opposed to the people who abandoned you, you can become a person who rises to the occasion and provides urgent aid when others need it. Many of the central characteristics of the Prophet ﷺ—which we pointed out earlier—include the attention and importance he gave to his Companions, the illuminating jokes he shared, and how he instilled a positive attitude within the people he spoke with. But an even greater trait which the Prophet ﷺ had was that he would never leave someone in their time of need, even if he himself was facing a similar predicament.

Even while being persecuted in Makkah and finding himself in dire straits, the Prophet ﷺ was always ready to help others. For instance, a man from a distant land came to the Prophet ﷺ and complained that the same people oppressing the Muslims owed him a debt which had not yet been repaid. Despite not knowing this man, the Prophet ﷺ went with him to the residence of the notorious enemy and torturer of Muslims known as Abū Jahl, and demanded that the man immediately receive his dues. If the Prophet ﷺ could do this for a man who he did not even know, one could imagine how much more he would fulfil for the people who he had established relationships with. Regarding this matter, Jābir ﷺ said: "The Prophet ﷺ was never asked for anything, to which he said 'no'." Instead, he ﷺ was always committed to do or say something to fulfil this person's needs. While it is true that he ﷺ would have to allocate his scarce time and resources to all claimants, he would never dismiss a particular request by leaving any person empty-handed. This can be clearly seen in how he ﷺ provided charity to the needy.

Even if someone was harsh or rude with him when attempting to take something from him, the Prophet never reciprocated. Anas ibn Mālik ﷺ narrated that the Prophet ﷺ was wearing a Najrānī cloak with a thick border. A Bedouin passed by them and tried to forcibly remove the mantle from the Prophet ﷺ. He was pulling so harshly that this left marks and bruises on the neck of the Prophet ﷺ. At the same time, the Bedouin was shouting to the Prophet:

أَعْطِنِي مِمَّا آتَاكَ الله

"Give to me from that which Allah has bestowed upon you."

In response, the Prophet ﷺ turned to the man, and simply smiled. He ﷺ then took off his mantle and gave it to the Bedouin. In fact, Anas ﷺ notes that the Prophet ﷺ ordered that the man be allotted a portion of charity (*ṣadaqah*) as well.

If someone asked the Prophet ﷺ for his help, he would always be available to provide his aid. It is important to note that his help was not restricted solely to the monetary realm, but extended to other matters as well. For instance, he ﷺ would intervene on behalf of anyone who sought his intercession. This was especially the case with orphans, as the Prophet ﷺ was aware of how vulnerable they were

If someone asked the Prophet ﷺ for his help, he would always be available to provide his aid. His help would even extend beyond the monetary realm to other areas such as resolving disputes, fulfilling debts and searching for a suitable spouse.

to exploitation. Even during the smallest of disputes, the Prophet ﷺ would be asked to intervene and mediate with his infinite wisdom. If there was a territory dispute between neighbours concerning the dividing line for their adjacent plots of land, the Prophet ﷺ would often arbitrate between the sides and help defuse tensions. Likewise, if you owed a debt which you were unable to pay, the Prophet ﷺ would always try to help. If he could not produce the required amount himself, the Prophet ﷺ would go to the lender and request leniency or debt forgiveness on your behalf. Furthermore, if you planned to get married, the Prophet ﷺ would search for a suitable spouse for you. For already married couples, the Prophet ﷺ would resolve disputes that would arise between husbands and wives.

Many of these cases did not involve the senior or high-ranking Companions; nor were many of the actors from the people of nobility. But this did not matter for the Prophet ﷺ, as he considered all these cases involving his brothers and sisters in need. He ﷺ always responded to a plea for support, regardless of the petitioner's status or rank. He ﷺ considered this type of service to the community to be a form of worship to Allah. It is in fact narrated that the Prophet ﷺ said:

وَلَأَنْ أَمْشِيَ مَعَ أَخٍ فِي حَاجَةٍ أَحَبُّ إِلَيَّ مِنْ أَنْ أَعْتَكِفَ
فِي هَذَا الْمَسْجِدِ شَهْرًا

"For me to go out and to help my brother in need is
more beloved than secluding myself in this masjid
for an entire month."

Think about the gravity and weight of this hadith.

One of the beautiful hadiths which illustrate how
he constantly served the community is narrated by
ʿAbdullāh ibn Abī Awfā ﷺ, where he said about the
Prophet ﷺ:

وَلَا يَأْنَفُ أَنْ يَمْشِيَ مَعَ الْأَرْمَلَةِ وَالْمِسْكِينِ فَيَقْضِيَ لَهُ الْحَاجَةَ

"He never was prideful to be seen walking with the
widow and orphan, and would accompany them
until he fulfilled their need."

The Prophet ﷺ was commonly seen helping others
by carrying their heavy loads. Likewise, he ﷺ would
accompany the weak and elderly and help them
carry their foodstuffs from the market. He ﷺ would
constantly undertake these tasks, despite these acts
being customarily considered low. But in the Prophet's
view, these acts were honourable and rewarding.

There is a beautiful narration in this matter, and it
reveals many valuable insights regarding the character

of the Prophet ﷺ. We often hear of this narration in paraphrased form, but it deserves to be recited in full. Anas ﷺ said that a woman who suffered from a mental illness (*fī ʿaqlihā shay'*) approached the Prophet ﷺ. She said:

يَا رَسُولَ اللهِ إِنَّ لِي إِلَيْكَ حَاجَةٌ

"O Messenger of Allah, I need your help for something."

The Prophet ﷺ could have easily dismissed her and ignored her call, but instead he ﷺ responded with full love and attention:

يَا أُمَّ فُلَانٍ، خُذِي أَيَّ الطُّرُقِ شِئْتِ، فَقُومِي فِيهِ حَتَّى أَقُومَ مَعَكِ

"O mother of So-and-so! Choose any path you want me to be in, and I will go there with you."

Practically, the Prophet ﷺ told her that regardless of what or where her need in question was, he would be present to help her. In essence, as Anas ﷺ mentioned:

فَخَلَا مَعَهَا فِي بَعْضِ الطُّرُقِ، حَتَّى فَرَغَتْ مِنْ حَاجَتِهَا

"He accompanied her on a road until she finished from her need."

She could take the Prophet ﷺ to any place she wanted to in the city of Madinah. This was the most important

person in Madinan society, yet this woman could order him to come with her anywhere she wanted, regardless of her needs. Yet, the Prophet ﷺ never complained of this nor did he remove his comforting smile towards her. He ﷺ never considered this woman to be insignificant, and did not protest that these requested services were a burden.

13

When No One Else Noticed

ome people spend their entire lives trying to come
to terms with injustices that others have inflicted
upon them. This causes them to pose many questions,
such as: "Why was I caused so much pain by this
person?" In addition, they may ask: "Why did I
have to go through this?" These types of queries are
understandable, since in this world, one may never
find a satisfactory and logical explanation. Another
group of people will accept the suffering that they have
experienced and instead aspire to become a source
of healing for the pain of others. In the case of the
Prophet ﷺ, it is well known that he underwent every
form of hardship imaginable, regardless of whether
it was rejection, financial dependency, or emotional
vulnerability. Because of his past experiences, he ﷺ
recognised the exact dynamics of every form of pain
and vulnerability. As a result of that, unlike others who

might have failed to notice, he had the full skillset to recognise when others were facing episodes of suffering.

Allah ﷻ says in the Qur'an:

حَقٌّ لِّلسَّآئِلِ وَالْمَحْرُوْمِ

"...there was a rightful share for the beggar and the poor." [5]

This verse means that the worshippers who pray at night must give their wealth as a right to the beggars and those who are in need, despite them not even asking. What this verse indicates is that there are two categories of the needy: people who will ask you for help when they are in pain, and others who will be forbidden from asking. The latter category may not vocally ask for help, sometimes as a result of their dignity, shame, or other circumstances. People who pray privately at night and give additional devotion to Allah are given a special lens to identify people who are in need, even if they do not verbally seek your help. Individuals who do not pray at night will not be blessed with this special form of intuition.

The Prophet ﷺ excelled at fulfilling the imperative found in this verse: he met the needs of those who

---

[5] *al-Dhāriyāt*, 19.

The Prophet ﷺ would never search for the hidden and shameful shortcomings of people ('awrāt). He ﷺ would not investigate the private matters of individuals. He ﷺ also shunned any vain, harmful, or prohibited speech, such as backbiting or gossip.

verbally asked, as well as the individuals who were prohibited from asking due to their circumstances.

'Alī ﷺ mentioned that the Prophet ﷺ provided the people relief in three matters. First, he ﷺ would never degrade or abuse people. This means that whenever he ﷺ made mention of an individual, he would never speak about them in a denigrating way. Secondly, the Prophet ﷺ would never search for the hidden and shameful shortcomings of people (*'awrāt*). In other words, he ﷺ would not investigate the private matters of individuals. Unfortunately, it is all too common to find individuals who consistently engage in this type of behaviour, such that they both pursue and expose the hidden shortcomings of people (*tatabbu' al-'awrāt*). The Prophet ﷺ would never engage in such matters, and in fact prohibited people from doing so. The third thing which 'Alī ﷺ mentioned is that the Prophet ﷺ would never speak except in circumstances which he hoped to be rewarded for. This means that he ﷺ shunned any vain, harmful, or prohibited speech, such as backbiting or gossip. Likewise, he ﷺ would never initiate conversations which would cause the other side to feel ashamed or embarrassed. Instead, he ﷺ would always ask about others in a manner which indicated his concern. If a person was not present, instead of asking unnecessary questions regarding them, he ﷺ would denote his anxiety about their absence by asking a simple and straightforward question such as, "Have you heard about that person? I have not seen them."

The Prophet ﷺ also had the aptitude to detect subtle things which others could not notice. Abū Hurayrah ؓ has this moving narration where he mentions that on one occasion his state of hunger was so intense that he would often faint. To alleviate the pain, he would tie stones to his stomach. He was in fact homeless for a period of time, and was a member of the Ahl al-Ṣuffah. Because of his strong sense of dignity, he was too ashamed to ask anyone for help or sustenance.

Instead of directly asking people for help, he ؓ attempted to pose questions to people, out of the hope that they would notice that he was in need of charity. Abū Hurayrah ؓ first went to Abū Bakr ؓ and tried to attract his attention. Abū Bakr was undoubtedly the best person after the Prophet ﷺ, and was known for his generosity, nobility, and kindness. He experienced some of the most difficult and epoch-shaping events with the Prophet ﷺ.

Abū Hurayrah ؓ posed to Abū Bakr ؓ a question about the interpretation of a verse found in the Book of Allah. Abū Hurayrah already knew the answer, but his intent was to have Abū Bakr notice his sense of hunger. As amazing as he was, Abū Bakr simply answered the question in a casual manner and proceeded on his way. So Abū Hurayrah proceeded to seek someone else's attention: ʿUmar ibn al-Khaṭṭāb ﷺ. Despite his eminent rank, ʿUmar simply answered Abū Hurayrah's question as well and did not notice his desperate state.

Abū Hurayrah ﷺ now felt helpless, as he had failed to draw anyone's attention to his state of hunger. He was in a state of despair, as his questions had not been effective in causing anyone to take note of his state. At this point, it is important to pause and reflect on this story. In many circumstances, we may see some of our friends make subtle cries for help, or say things which indicate that they may be facing serious problems in life. It is incorrect to ignore those warning signs and move on as if they are nothing of significance. If you truly love those individuals, you should be concerned and take any necessary steps to provide aid and ensure that they are fine.

Continuing with our story, Abū Hurayrah ﷺ remained in a serious state of hunger. It seemed that nobody would notice that he urgently needed food. But then the Prophet ﷺ walked by Abū Hurayrah and observed his state. He looked at Abū Hurayrah, smiled towards him, and said: "O Abū Hirr!" The Prophet ﷺ instilled a sense of ease and comfort in Abū Hurayrah's heart by using a shortened version of his nickname. In response, Abū Hurayrah immediately said: "I am at your service (*labbayk*), O Messenger of Allah!" He wanted to know if the Prophet ﷺ was in need of any services or help. The Prophet ﷺ said: "Follow me." Abū Hurayrah said: "So I followed the Prophet. He took me to this person's house, where we were served with milk (*laban*). The Prophet ﷺ took the pitcher of milk and passed it around the room, so everybody could drink from it. I was worried that nothing would be left for me once my turn arrived. Once it finally reached me, the Prophet ﷺ said: 'Drink, O Abū Hurayrah.'"

Abū Hurayrah ﷺ continued to drink for an extended period of time, and kept the pitcher locked with his lips. He proceeded to consume from it until he could drink no more. Then the Prophet ﷺ said: "O Abū Hirr!" Abū Hurayrah said in response: "I am at your service, O Messenger of Allah!" The Prophet ﷺ said: "Are you full?" Abū Hurayrah replied in the affirmative. So the Prophet ﷺ took the pitcher from him and drank from it as well.

We learn from this story that the Prophet ﷺ was able to easily observe the pain, hunger, or despair that others underwent. This is because throughout his life, he ﷺ had gone through all of these different forms of difficulties. He ﷺ had faced rejection, betrayal, and mockery from others. For this reason, the Prophet ﷺ ensured that he would always be a source of comfort for individuals who went through such trials and misfortunes.

There was a man who would frequently attend the gatherings and sessions of the Prophet ﷺ. This man would also bring his son to the *masjid*, who he loved and adored a lot. The Prophet ﷺ and his Companions would even play with this child.

Suddenly, this man no longer attended the Prophet's gatherings, and was not seen in the *masjid*. The Prophet ﷺ asked his Companions about the condition of this man. The Companions said: "His son…" The Prophet ﷺ said: "What happened to his son?" The Companions explained that the man's son had passed away. In response, the Prophet ﷺ said that they should all go and visit him. During their visit, they found the man to be intensely sad. They asked him what had happened, and he explained that he was still mourning the loss of his son. It is at this point that the Prophet ﷺ said: "Are you not pleased to know that on the Day of Judgement you will find your son in front of every gate of Paradise, and you will be allowed to enter through any gate that you choose?" *Subḥānallāh*, what glad tidings! The man was visibly shocked to hear this wonderful news. He replied,

"Of course, O Messenger of Allah!" He then asked:
"Is this just for me, or for everyone?" The Prophet ﷺ
replied by stating that this glad tiding and gift will be
for the whole *ummah*.

Reflect on this story, especially on how it is noted that
the Prophet ﷺ searched and visited the man himself.
He actively looked for people suffering from hunger,
sadness, rejection, and other misfortunes. He helped
these people without them even needing to ask, since
he was the epitome of religious excellence (*iḥsan*).

The Prophet ﷺ was able to easily observe the pain, hunger, or despair that others underwent because he ﷺ had gone through different forms of difficulties in his life. He ﷺ had faced rejection, betrayal, and mockery from others so he ﷺ would always be a source of comfort for individuals who went through such trials and misfortunes.

14

When He Was Angry

If you are a person who is always angry, it is likely that your peers will dismiss you as being hot tempered. On matters of a serious nature, people will not value your opinion or passion, as they know you are always of that temperament. However, if you are a person who is largely of a cheerful disposition, then your anger will be taken seriously. This is because in this latter circumstance people are aware of the fact that you do not become angry over petty or trifle matters. In fact, there is an aphorism in the Arabic language which states:

اتَّقِ غَضَبَ الحَليمِ

"Beware of the anger of the forbearing person."

The upshot of this saying is that the anger of a typically cheerful person is significant, as it indicates a red line has been crossed. This is because such a person does not customarily become angry. In contrast, one of the signs of the hypocrite is that they often become aggressive and angry. According to the Prophet ☙, one of the signs of the hypocrite is that:

وَإِذَا خَاصَمَ فَجَرَ

"...when they argue, they become belligerent."

Hypocrites always transgress their limits in the midst of an argument by taking an aggressive line, and never listen to the advising party. Regarding this matter, the Prophet ☙ said that the worst of people are those who nobody seeks to advise anymore, since they are afraid of dealing with their vile attitude (*fuḥsh*). When someone is so hot-tempered and falls into fits of rage whenever they are corrected, eventually everyone will abandon them and cease advising them anymore. Such a person will eventually be fully deprived of sincere religious advice (*naṣīḥah*), and will actually harm themselves the most. They will make everything and everyone around them unpleasant. In the process, they will lack self-awareness of the blameworthy qualities that they have and should rectify immediately. Regarding the dangerous nature of anger, ʿAlī ☙ has a very powerful statement:

أَوَّلَهُ جُنُونٌ وَآخِرَهُ نَدَمُ

"Its initial stage is craziness, while its end is full of regret."

People that go through fits of anger start off crazy and end up regretful. May Allah help and rehabilitate anyone who seeks to treat their anger issues.

When we look at the Prophet's conduct ﷺ, he never was foul (*fāḥish*) in his statements, nor did he become angry over worldly matters. He ﷺ never denigrated others, nor did he use a dismissive tone against the people. Instead, his anger was carefully composed and channeled, as it was always harnessed to achieve valid objectives. This is because if your anger is for the sake of Allah and you are advancing a righteous cause, you cannot be characterised with the manners of Shayṭān. If your anger is due to your love for Allah, then it must abide by the principles and objectives that Allah has mandated. This was the way of all the Prophets. You find this form of principled anger when Musā ﷺ found his people worshipping the golden calf. The same can be said when 'Īsā ﷺ dealt with the money changers in the temple.

The Prophet ✾ used to beautifully invoke Allah
by saying:

اللَّهُمَّ إِنِّي أَسْأَلُكَ كَلِمَةَ الْحَقِّ فِي الرِّضَا والْغَضَبِ

*"O Allah, I ask from you the ability to speak the word
of truth in times of pleasure and anger."*

This *du'ā'* is full of many valuable insights. It points
to the fact that in times of anger, it becomes difficult
to maintain control over one's own personality.
Instead, an angry person allows forces of evil to take
over them. For this reason, the Prophet ✾ is pointing
to the importance of returning back to the truth
(*ḥaqq*), since that is what our lives and personalities
must revolve around.

How did the Prophet act when he became angry?
'Ā'ishah ✾ and other Companions provide a vivid
portrayal of the Prophet's conduct when he ✾
became angry:

وَمَا انْتَقَمَ رَسُوْلُ اللهِ صَلَّى اللهُ عَلَيْهِ وَسَلَّمَ لِنَفْسِهِ فِي شَيْءٍ قَطُّ،
إِلَّا أَنْ تُنْتَهَكَ حُرْمَةُ اللهِ، فَيَنْتَقِمَ بِهَا لِلهِ

*"The Messenger of Allah ✾ never got angry for
himself, unless if Allah's sacred boundaries and
prohibitions were violated; in such a case he
would seek revenge for the sake of Allah."*

Once someone crossed the boundaries, the Prophet ﷺ
would get angry for Allah's sake. That was likely
very difficult to see from the Prophet ﷺ, as it was
not the norm. We see this type of anger activated
with Usāmah ibn Zayd ﷺ, who the Prophet ﷺ loved
immensely. However, this Companion killed a fighter
in the battlefield, despite this person saying the
testimony of faith (*shahādah*) right before Usāmah
struck him. Usāmah ﷺ reasoned that this person
only said the testimony due to the fear of death,
so he had not truly become a Muslim. When he
told the Prophet ﷺ about this event, the Prophet
became intensely angry. He ﷺ was so upset that he
repeatedly asked Usāmah: "Did you check his heart,
O Usāmah?" In fact, Usāmah said: "He was so upset
with me that I wished I had not become Muslim
before that day." He ﷺ meant by this statement that
he wished he could take the testimony of faith on
that day and do away with all wrongs before that.

We likewise have the story of the three young men
who came to the house of the Prophet and inquired
of his habits. When they found out that the Prophet ﷺ
slept sometimes at night, had marital relations with
his wives, and did not fast every day, they reasoned
that they should do more than him, since he was
after all the Messenger of Allah. As a result, one of
them vowed that they would fast every single day.

The Prophet ﷺ would become upset whenever a person was belittled or made fun of, since respect towards one's fellow Muslim is an issue of utmost importance. This matter also pertains to the rights of Allah, since it is He who enshrines the sanctity and dignity of every individual Muslim.

The second stated that they would remain awake the whole night in prayer. The third person stated that they would never have marital relations with women and would not marry. When the Prophet ﷺ found out about the oaths that they took, he became upset. He informed them angrily that he was the Messenger of Allah, and no one would be able to exceed him in religiosity. He ﷺ further stated to them: "Yet I fast intermittently, I sleep, and I marry women. Whoever turns away from my Sunnah is not from me."

Hence, these are the areas where the Prophet ﷺ would become upset, namely whenever people tried to deface aspects of the religion or exceeded the boundaries of Allah. Likewise, the Prophet ﷺ would become upset whenever a person was belittled or made fun of, since respect towards one's fellow Muslim is an issue of utmost importance. This matter also pertains to the rights of Allah, since it is He who enshrines the sanctity and dignity of every individual Muslim. For instance, when the Companions made fun of ʿAbdullāh ibn Masʿūd's legs and pointed out how skinny they were, the Prophet ﷺ became extremely upset. In defending Ibn Masʿūd ﷺ, he said: "By Him in whose Hand is my soul! His legs will weigh heavier on the Scales than Mount Uḥud on the Day of Judgement." In essence, he ﷺ was pointing to the fact that his legs were legs of honour and power in the sight of Allah.

Likewise, many of us are aware of the famous story of Abū Dharr ✤, who once cursed Bilāl ✤ by calling him *ibn al-sawdā'*, which means son of a black woman. The Prophet ✻ became extremely upset, and addressed Abū Dharr by saying: "Did you insult him by insulting his mother? Indeed, you are a person that still has some aspects of the Days of Ignorance (*jāhiliyyah*) inside of you."

We notice that whenever the sacred boundaries were crossed, the Prophet ✻ took swift and decisive action to address the wrongs committed. Perhaps the greatest illustration of this type of intervention came with ʿĀishah ✤, where the Prophet ✻ became extremely upset with her. ʿĀishah ✤ found it peculiar that the Prophet ✻ would always mention and praise Khadījah ✤, as if he loved no one in the entire world more than her. This was despite the fact that she had passed away many years prior; ʿĀishah had never seen her and was curious as to why her name was always mentioned. Every time the Prophet ✻ saw some of her friends or loved ones, he sent gifts to them. Likewise, whenever he heard the voice of someone who sounded like her sister Hālah, he would become immensely pleased and say: "O Allah, let it be Hālah! O Allah, let it be Hālah!"

ʿĀishah ✤ states that on occasion, she made the following comment: "I said to the Prophet ✻ as he was remembering Khadījah: 'Why do you preoccupy yourself with an old and toothless woman from Quraysh, while Allah has replaced her with someone better?'" Upon saying that, 'Ā'ishah knew she crossed the line. Immediately, the Prophet ﷺ stood up, and his face became red. The vein on his face which would reveal itself during his state of anger had bulged. In fact, the Prophet was so upset that it appeared as if all his hair stood up.

مَا أَبْدَلَنِي اللهُ عَزَّ وَجَلَّ خَيْرًا مِنْهَا، قَدْ آمَنَتْ بِي إِذْ كَفَرَ بِي النَّاسُ، وَصَدَّقَتْنِي إِذْ كَذَّبَنِي النَّاسُ، وَوَاسَتْنِي بِمَالِهَا إِذْ حَرَمَنِي النَّاسُ، وَرَزَقَنِي اللهُ عَزَّ وَجَلَّ وَلَدَهَا إِذْ حَرَمَنِي أَوْلَادَ النِّسَاءِ

"Allah has never given me anyone better than her. She believed in me when others disbelieved in me, and considered me truthful when the people called me a liar. She spent on me when others deprived me, and Allah provided me children with her, while He did not allow that to happen with any other woman."

The Prophet ﷺ beautifully enumerated all the different factors which rendered Khadījah ﷺ to be irreplaceable. After hearing the Prophet's statement, 'Ā'ishah ﷺ immediately apologised, and promised that she would never speak about Khadījah again. The Prophet ﷺ accepted her apology and forgave her. The Prophet ﷺ could have censured her harshly for her criticism of Khadījah, but he instead did something far more beautiful. Instead of criticising ʿĀʾishah and pointing out why she is inferior to Khadījah, he ✾ focused on the unique qualities which made Khadījah superior. The reason why the Prophet ✾ undertook this course of action was that he did not want to denigrate anyone; instead, his sole objective was to protect the honour of Khadījah. He ✾ only became upset because Khadījah was not given the respect and recognition she deserved.

15

When He
Saw Oppression

If a person becomes indifferent to injustice, that
indicates a strong deficiency in their faith (*īmān*).
Whenever the Prophet ﷺ saw someone get wronged,
he would immediately address the predicament
by taking any necessary measures. He ﷺ had an
immense hatred towards oppression; that was because
the Prophet ﷺ loved what Allah ﷻ loved, and hated
what Allah ﷻ hated. Allah has explicitly stated that
He hates oppression, and has made it forbidden for us.
So what would it be like when the Prophet ﷺ saw you
being wronged? Likewise, how would he ﷺ react if he
saw you wronging someone else in his presence?

The hadiths on this topic are so many that they cannot
in fact be enumerated. But perhaps one of the best
descriptions of the Prophet ﷺ in this regard came from
none other than Khadījah ﷺ, who said to the Prophet:

تُعِينُ عَلَى نَوَائِبِ الْحَقِّ

"You support anyone that serves a righteous and truthful cause."

By this all-inclusive statement, she ﷻ meant that the Prophet ﷺ provided support to anyone who had a righteous cause through any means possible, whether it was providing aid, financial resources, or emotional support. Likewise, this meant that whenever people were wronged and they had no one to advocate on their behalf, he ﷺ would be the one who would stand up and defend them. Amazingly, we note that Khadījah ﷻ made this statement before the Messenger ﷺ began his Prophetic mission. One can only imagine how much more the Prophet ﷺ was a defender of the oppressed after he had received the divine message from Allah.

Abū Masʿūd al-Badrī ﷻ has an interesting narration about himself. It is not a pleasant report, as Abū Masʿūd ﷻ is actually the wrongdoer in this scenario. Yet he narrated it so people could appreciate the lessons derived from this exhortation of the Prophet ﷺ. Likewise, by sharing this report, the *ummah* could derive numerous benefits and further appreciate the character of the Prophet ﷺ for centuries to come. In this story, Abū Masʿūd stated that he was physically disciplining his slave while in a fit of rage. He was continuously whipping this slave in a harsh and

The Prophet ﷺ did not ignore the call of the oppressed, even if no one else heard it. Even if others ignored the pleas of the oppressed or deemed their complaints to be insignificant, the Prophet ﷺ always answered their call.

horrifying manner. Then, suddenly, Abū Masʿūd heard a voice shouting his name:

اِعْلَمْ أَبَا مَسْعُودٍ اِعْلَمْ أَبَا مَسْعُودٍ اِعْلَمْ أَبَا مَسْعُودٍ

"Know, O Abū Masʿūd! Know, O Abū Masʿūd! Know, O Abū Masʿūd!"

The Prophet ❀ was continuously shouting the Companion's name. Yet as Abū Masʿūd ❀ noted, he was not able to recognise the person's voice due to the enraged state he was still in. Yet, as he heard the voice more closely, it dawned upon him that it was the Messenger of Allah ❀ who was addressing him. He was not used to hearing the Prophet's voice with such an intense tone. He turned towards the Prophet ❀ and noticed the anger in his face. After observing this scene, Abū Masʿūd dropped the whip from his hand. The Prophet ❀ then said to him:

اعْلَمْ، أَبَا مَسْعُودٍ، أَنَّ اللهَ أَقْدَرُ عَلَيْكَ مِنْكَ عَلَى هَذَا الْغُلَامِ

"Know, O Abū Masʿūd, that Allah has more authority over you than you have over this young servant!"

The Prophet ❀ emphasised to Abū Masʿūd ❀ the fact that Allah could discipline him in a far more capable manner than what he could do to this young man. Abū Masʿūd ❀ was shocked by the anger of the Prophet ❀, and how he stood up for this young man.

You find the Prophet ﷺ displaying the same firm line when he was informed of other cases of oppression in his community. In a narration reported by ʿAlī ibn Abī Ṭālib ؓ, a woman came to the Prophet ﷺ to complain about how she was being mistreated by her husband. As we know, women would often come to the Prophet ﷺ and seek his help if they were being mistreated by their spouses. In fact, *Surah al-Mujādilah* was revealed concerning a woman who sought a remedy for a difficult state she was put in by her husband. But in ʿAlī's report, the woman who came concealed herself to hide her identity. She complained to the Prophet ﷺ that her husband was beating her. The Prophet ﷺ told her: "Tell him that you are under the protection of the Messenger of Allah." What an amazing guarantee! She went to her husband and conveyed to him this message. However, she then came back and informed the Prophet ﷺ that he hit her again. The wording of the hadith suggests that she still did not want to reveal her identity. In response to her complaint, the Prophet ﷺ ripped off a piece of his shirt and gave it to the woman, ordering her to show it to him and reiterate his earlier statement. This was a physical piece of evidence that the Prophet ﷺ sought the protection of this wife. Some time later, the woman returned to the Prophet ﷺ and complained once again that her husband beat her. Now, the Prophet ﷺ raised his hands and made *duʿāʾ* against the husband, as a piece of his own shirt did not deter him.

The Prophet ✤ took this matter so seriously that he now asked Allah to take action against this man's continual oppression. You can see from this final measure that the Prophet ✤ took oppression very seriously, and continued to try to find a solution for the woman.

What is more amazing about the Prophet ✤ is that he could even hear the complaints of animals. Although we may not be able to understand their speech, the Prophet ✤ could understand their cries for help. During a war expedition, a bird hovered over the Prophet ✤ and the Companions and was furiously flapping its wings in distress. Despite the serious wartime context, the Prophet ✤ observed the bird and realised that it was facing a predicament. He turned to the Companions and asked:

مَنْ فَجَعَ هَذِهِ بِوَلَدِهَا

"Who has hurt this one with regards to her child?"

Ponder upon how this question has been beautifully phrased. If you did not know the background of the story, you would think that he ✤ was talking about an actual human, not a bird. But this shows how much outraged the Prophet ✤ had become, and how much pain he felt after seeing this bird fly around in this manner. One of the Companions then mentioned that they had taken some of this bird's chicks.

The Prophet ﷺ ordered that they be returned back to the mother's nest, so that they would be relieved.

There is yet another narration pertaining to this theme, and it also involves an animal. Sahl ibn 'Amr ؓ narrates that the Prophet ﷺ passed by a camel and noticed that it was so thin and frail that its stomach touched its back. This was because it was not fed and nourished properly by its owner. The Prophet ﷺ went to observe the animal, and found that it lacked weight. He ﷺ started to comfort it and then addressed the people by saying: "Fear Allah regarding these animals that do not speak. Ride them when they are in good condition and feed them when they are in good condition."

In other words, the Prophet ﷺ is informing us that just like how we ride and benefit from them while they are in good health, we should nourish and take care of them as well. He also noted that this camel was complaining to him regarding its deplorable state, and the Prophet ﷺ listened to it and even articulated its complaint on its behalf. Thus, we observe from these stories that the Prophet ﷺ did not ignore the call of the oppressed, even if no one else heard it. Even if everyone else ignored the pleas of the oppressed for help or deemed their complaints to be insignificant, the Prophet ﷺ always answered their call.

It's amazing that the Prophet ﷺ could even hear the complaints of animals. He ﷺ could understand their cries for help. He ﷺ noted that a camel was complaining to him regarding its malnourished state, and the Prophet ﷺ listened to it and even articulated its complaint on its behalf.

16

When You Thought He Cursed You

In general terms, to face criticism or disappointment from the people who you love the most is always a difficult matter. For instance, among your two parents, one of them might be extremely loving, patient, and forgiving towards you. If you ever cause that particular parent to become upset with you, that can be very difficult to bear. Likewise, if you have a teacher or friend that you really admire and are always trying to impress, it is painful the first time you make them upset. But there is a sensation of guilt and sadness that is worse than all these previous experiences put together. Imagine if you were cursed by the Prophet ﷺ, or you came to believe that he made *du'ā'* against you. When posing this hypothetical scenario, I am not talking about someone who was a fervent enemy of the Prophet ﷺ, who became Muslim later on. I am actually talking about you in particular. Imagine that you are a Muslim living in Madinah and you did something which angered or disappointed the Prophet ﷺ, such that you think that the Prophet ﷺ made *du'ā'* against you. How would you react to that, and would you even be able to recover from such a stunning situation?

Even when it came to the enemies of Islam, the Prophet ﷺ did not generally curse people, even if they made derogatory comments against him. In a beautiful hadith, the Prophet ﷺ is confirmed to have said:

إِنِّي لَمْ أُبْعَثْ لَعَّانًا وَإِنَّمَا بُعِثْتُ رَحْمَةً

"I was not sent to curse people, but I was only sent as a mercy."

This means that in general terms, the Prophet ﷺ refrained from cursing his enemies. In the rare circumstances which he did, it was only done against specific individuals, such as the leading belligerents in the Battle of Badr. All these leaders were killed in the battlefield and buried in the same ditch. However, this was rarely done. In the overwhelming majority of cases, when the Prophet ﷺ was asked to curse a particular tribe or people, he would instead supplicate that they be guided.

I would like to share a few stories that involve Muslims, and relate to members of the *ummah*. The first example

Even when it came to the enemies of Islam, the Prophet ﷺ did not generally curse people, even if they made derogatory comments against him. In a beautiful hadith, he ﷺ is confirmed to have said: "I was not sent to curse people, but I was only sent as a mercy."

is particularly touching, and one that is very near to my heart. Anas ibn Mālik ✦ related that an orphan girl lived under the guardianship of Umm Sulaym ✦. One day the Prophet ✦ visited the latter's house, and also met the orphan girl. He addressed the girl and said:

أَنْتِ هِيَ؟

"Are you her?"

By this question, the Prophet ✦ was pointing to the fact that he had not seen the girl for a period of time, and did not immediately recognise her. He was amazed that the girl had grown so much, which is why he ✦ then said:

لَقَدْ كَبِرْتِ لَا كَبِرَ سِنُّكِ

"You have grown so much! May you not get any older."

This was a beautiful idiomatic expression denoting his surprise with how much the girl had grown since the last time he saw her. Sometimes, we may use similar expressions as well. For instance, you may have seen your friend's young daughter or relative grow up greatly in a short amount of time, so you say: "Wow, you have grown so much! You need to stop growing on me!" Informally speaking, such an expression is used to denote one's amazement with a person's pace of growth.

Sadly, this young girl seems to have misunderstood the intended meaning of the Prophet's statement, and interpreted it to mean that the Prophet ﷺ had made *du'ā'* against her. As a result, she goes home and weeps profusely. Umm Sulaym ؓ noticed her sadness, and asked her: "O my dear daughter, what is wrong with you?" The girl replied: "The Prophet of Allah made *du'ā'* against me." The young girl had interpreted the Prophet's supplication to mean one of two things. The first interpretation was that she would die immediately. Otherwise, the girl thought that she would stay the same size, and would never grow up. She was frightened of the possibility of dying or staying at the same age without changing at all. Umm Sulaym ؓ realised that something was wrong, as she was very close with the Prophet ﷺ and knew his character well. She knew for a fact that the Prophet ﷺ loved the orphans, and deeply displayed affection towards children. In order to find out the truth, Umm Sulaym ؓ quickly donned her *ḥijāb* and rushed towards the residence of the Prophet ﷺ. She came with such urgency that the Prophet ﷺ asked her:

يَا أُمَّ سُلَيْمٍ مَا لَكِ

"O Umm Sulaym, what is wrong?"

Umm Sulaym ✺ said in response: "O Messenger of
Allah, did you supplicate against my orphan girl?"
The Prophet ✺ said back to her, "O Umm Sulaym,
how is that so?" To this, Umm Sulaym ✺ said: "She
claimed that you supplicated against her, and now
she will never grow in age." After hearing this, the
Prophet ✺ started to laugh, and then said:

يَا أُمَّ سُلَيْمٍ أَمَا تَعْلَمِينَ أَنَّ شَرْطِي عَلَى رَبِّي أَنِّي اشْتَرَطْتُ عَلَى رَبِّي فَقُلْتُ إِنَّمَا
أَنَا بَشَرٌ أَرْضَى كَمَا يَرْضَى الْبَشَرُ وَأَغْضَبُ كَمَا يَغْضَبُ الْبَشَرُ فَأَيُّمَا أَحَدٍ
دَعَوْتُ عَلَيْهِ مِنْ أُمَّتِي بِدَعْوَةٍ لَيْسَ لَهَا بِأَهْلٍ أَنْ تَجْعَلَهَا لَهُ طَهُورًا وَزَكَاةً
وَقُرْبَةً يُقَرِّبُهُ بِهَا مِنْهُ يَوْمَ الْقِيَامَةِ

*"O Umm Sulaym, do you not know of the condition
that I set with my Lord? The condition which I set
is that I said [to Him]: 'I am a mortal human and
I become pleased like how they become pleased
and I become angry like how they become angry.
So whenever I make du'ā' against a member of my
ummah who does not deserve of it, I ask that it be
made a source of purification and nearness to Him
on the Day of Judgement.'"*

Through this rich and comprehensive explanation, the
Prophet ✺ had settled the matter. Even if his expression
was read literally and at its formal meaning, Allah
had granted the Prophet ✺ his wish: if he ever made
a negative supplication against a Muslim who did not
deserve it, Allah will convert it to a reward for them.

While the aforementioned story occurred due to a serious misunderstanding, there are other cases where the Prophet ﷺ genuinely cursed someone. This is also perhaps a story which many people have not heard of. It is a far more serious episode which most interestingly involves ʿĀʾishah ﷺ as a character. As ʿĀʾishah ﷺ relates, in the aftermath of a battle, the Prophet ﷺ brought one of the prisoners of war to his household. He issued explicit orders to her that the prisoner should be supervised carefully at all times, lest he escape. He mentioned that she should exercise extreme caution and not lose sight of him. This was undoubtedly a very sensitive and dangerous situation, as the post-war climate was still tense and unstable. To restore order and calm to the scene, it was imperative that any prisoners and other potential sources of danger be supervised carefully. After issuing these instructions, the Prophet ﷺ left ʿĀʾishah ﷺ. But then, some of ʿĀʾishah's friends came over to visit, and she began to engage in a conversation with them. She became so engrossed with her friends and socialised indulgently to the extent that she actually forgot about the prisoner. By the time she remembered and rushed to check the room in which the prisoner was held, he had already disappeared. A short time later, the Prophet ﷺ returned and discovered that the prisoner was missing. He asked ʿĀʾishah ﷺ: "What happened with the prisoner?" She said in response:

"I became distracted from supervising him after my
female friends came." The Prophet ﷺ then said:

قَطَعَ اللهُ يَدَكِ

"May Allah cut your hand."

This was once again an idiomatic expression, which
was not intended literally. Immediately after saying
this, the Prophet ﷺ left the house to pursue this
fugitive. The situation had escalated seriously, as a
dangerous combatant who just recently engaged in
hostilities was free outside in Madinan society and
could harm anyone. ʿĀʾishah ﷺ remained at home,
in a state of shock and despair. Even though the
Prophet's statement was non-literal, ʿĀʾishah ﷺ was
aware of the Prophet's miracles and powerful signs,
and believed that something bad would happen to her.
Later in the day, the Prophet ﷺ returned home and
saw ʿĀʾishah ﷺ sitting in the living room, turning and
carefully observing her hands (*tuqallib yadayhā*) with
fear. The Prophet ﷺ said:

مَا لَكِ، أُجُنِنْتِ

"What is wrong with you, have you gone insane?"

ʿĀʾishah ﷺ said in response: "You supplicated against
me, so I am turning my hands to see which one
of them will be cut off." The Prophet ﷺ dispelled

'Ā'ishah's fears by reminding her that if he ever says something like that against a member of his *ummah*, he has asked Allah to make that instead a source of purification for them. As a result, she had no reason to worry about one of her hands falling off. The Prophet ﷺ then followed his comforting response with a beautiful *duʿāʾ*:

اللَّهُمَّ فَأَيُّمَا مُؤْمِنٍ سَبَبْتُهُ، فَاجْعَلْ ذَلِكَ لَهُ قُرْبَةً إِلَيْكَ يَوْمَ القِيَامَةِ

"O Allah, if there is any believer who I curse, then make that expression a means of allowing them to be close to you on the Day of Judgement."

Thus, when he used such an expression against someone due to anger or a similar reason, he ensured that it was still a form of mercy for them and a source of purification.

Allah had granted
the Prophet ﷺ his wish:
if he ever made a negative
supplication against a
Muslim who did not
deserve it, Allah will convert
it to a reward for them.
Thus he ﷺ ensured that it
was still a form of mercy
for them and a source
of purification.

If You Claimed
He Hurt You

If you are generally a merciful person, then this implies that if someone comes to you and tells you that you hurt their feelings, you will immediately listen to them. You will likely lend this person an ear by allowing them to voice their grievances. Imagine then how attentive the Prophet ﷺ would be if someone informed him that he somehow hurt him?

As confirmed numerous times in this series, the Prophet ﷺ had a strong degree of emotional intelligence, such that he could intuitively perceive things. He was able to know if someone was upset with him. He once said to ʿĀʾishah ﷺ: "I can tell when you are angry with me, even if you do not directly tell me." She asked: "How is that so?" The Prophet ﷺ said: "This is because when you are pleased with me, you swear by saying, 'By the Lord of Muhammad'.

But when you are upset with me, you swear by saying, 'By the Lord of Ibrāhīm'." So whenever she ❦ did not mention his name, the Prophet ❦ knew that something was wrong.

So the Prophet ❦ could sense a person's displeasure or discomfort with him. Out of his mercy and kindness, he ❦ would ask you if something was wrong and if he could help alleviate the situation. Even in tense and high-stake circumstances, we notice that the Prophet ❦ was held to a higher standard which he himself was committed to uphold. One of the famous stories concerning this theme involves ʿAbdullāh ibn Umm Maktūm ❦, which is mentioned in the beginning of *Surah ʿAbasa*. This is a short chapter found in *Juzʾ ʿAmma*, the last section of the Qurʾan. All of us—including our children—are aware of this chapter and have likely memorised it; it mentions that the Prophet ❦ frowned towards a blind man. The background for this story is that ʿAbdullāh ibn Umm Maktūm ❦ quickly rushed towards the Prophet ❦ and asked him to teach him from the religion. When the Prophet ❦ saw ʿAbdullāh ibn Umm Maktūm ❦ approaching him, he frowned. This is because the Prophet ❦ was in the midst of a serious discussion with the elite members of Quraysh, who were showing interest in Islam for the first time. The Prophet ❦ felt that he finally had the chance to talk to them and have them potentially join

the faith. But 'Abdullāh ibn Umm Maktūm's arrival
and interruption spoiled this opportunity, since he
was from the poorer and lower strata of society. Since
he was blind, he could not notice the gravity of the
situation. What aggravated the matter was that Ibn
Umm Maktūm was shouting towards the Prophet ﷺ,
"O Messenger of Allah, teach me from what Allah
taught you." Upon hearing this address, the Prophet ﷺ
frowned and continued his conversation with the elites.
As a result of what happened, Allah revealed this
surah to gently admonish the Prophet ﷺ, correct him
for this oversight, and hold him to a higher standard.
From that point onwards, the Prophet ﷺ would always
treat 'Abdullāh ibn Umm Maktūm ﷺ in a respected
and dignified manner by saying:

مَرْحَبًا بِمَنْ عَاتَبَنِي فِيهِ رَبِّي

"Welcome to he on behalf of whom Allah admonished
me."

So the Prophet ﷺ would issue him this special greeting,
and would honour him since the revelation of that chapter.
He ensured that 'Abdullāh ibn Umm Maktūm ﷺ had
a unique rank in the community. On some occasions,
he allowed him to give the call of prayer (*adhān*) in the
place of Bilāl ﷺ. Furthermore, despite his inability to
engage in battles due to his blindness, the Prophet ﷺ still
appointed him as a flag-bearer. In essence, the Prophet ﷺ

ensured that that he would have a productive role in all different facets and spheres of society. Ultimately, the Prophet's frown actually ended up having immense blessings for this Companion.

There was yet another incident that occurred during a high-stake situation: war. As Usayd ibn Ḥuḍayr ♔ narrates, the Prophet ♔ was once walking by the ranks of his soldiers and troops, and ensured that they were lined up properly. During this tense moment, there was a young man from the Helpers who was constantly making funny statements and causing the people to laugh. One can imagine how unacceptable this was: just as people are getting ready for a battle, a person is failing to appreciate the seriousness of the situation and causing others to laugh. The Prophet ♔ poked this young man under his ribcage with his staff to discipline him and put him in line. Since he was the leader of the military, the Prophet ♔ had every right to ensure all the soldiers were obedient and observing the correct behaviour before the battle began.

Surprisingly, the young man immediately responded back to the Prophet ♔ by saying: "Let me retaliate (*aṣbirnī*)." The man believed that he had the right to hit the Prophet ♔ in return. At this point, the Prophet ♔ could have simply dismissed his claim and moved on. In fact, he could have even further admonished the young man for crossing his limits and daring to make such a suggestion. Even more so, he could have explained why he poked him in the first place, which was self-evident and fully justifiable in everyone's view. It was solely done to pacify him and ensure he did not act as a nuisance and disturb the rest of the soldiers.

However, after the man made this demand, the Prophet ﷺ approached him and asked him to take his retaliation. Reflect on this level of humility. The Prophet ﷺ did not say anything: he did not dismiss the man, nor did he attempt to justify his actions. He could have belittled the man by asking him to leave the army ranks, or tell him to defer the matter until the war's aftermath. Instead, he responded positively to the man's command and granted him his wish. This young man then said to the Prophet ﷺ:

إِنَّ عَلَيْكَ قَمِيصًا وَلَيْسَ عَلَيَّ قَمِيصٌ

"You are wearing a shirt, while I am not."

By this statement, he meant that since his skin was exposed, the Prophet's strike left a mark and hurt him. But the Prophet's body was covered, which implied that he ﷺ would not experience the same degree of pain if the man struck him in retaliation. The Prophet ﷺ could have simply ignored this objection, and ordered the man to simply poke him

with his garment on. But instead, he ※ complied
with the man's demand and raised his shirt. Just
imagine that you are witnessing this scene right now!
How would you react when you see the Prophet's
humbleness and lack of vanity? But after the
Prophet ※ did this, the man hugged the Prophet,
kissed his ribs, and then said:

إِنَّمَا أُرِدْتُ هَذَا يَا رَسُولَ اللهِ

"I only wanted this, O Messenger of Allah."

Throughout this whole exchange we can derive many
rich insights. It reveals that the Prophet ※ was so
humble that he ensured that anyone who felt that
they were wronged by him could have recourse to a
full remedy. But the more he ※ gave such concessions
and remedies, the more he made the people love him.
Furthermore, through these actions he ※ elevated
himself in honour and rank.

18

When You Sought His Forgiveness

A t an individual level, there is a negative correlation between how much grudges and grievances you hold in your heart towards people in the night, and how much love you can have towards your Creator. If you are full of hatred towards others, then you will not be able to ascend to the highest rank in the sight of your Lord. This is the wisdom behind the hadith where the Prophet ﷺ emphasised that a man was from the people of Paradise, as during the night he would empty his heart of all grudges and forgive anyone who had wronged him. Likewise, the Prophet ﷺ could never hold any grudge against anyone in his heart when he was so busy nurturing it with the love of Allah during every single night. This is the reason why you never find the Prophet ﷺ bringing up any past grievances. Neither do you find him burdening himself or others with previous grudges, despite him being surrounded with people who had attempted to assassinate him or were responsible for the murders of his family members and Companions.

It is likely the case that if you were a Companion of the Prophet ﷺ, you would have exceeded your boundaries occasionally when addressing him. This was because the Prophet was so humble, soft, and merciful that a person would sometimes overstep the necessary limits in their conduct towards him, such as raising their voice. Likewise, a person might have taken advantage of his generosity and kindness. But if a Companion realised that they went too far in a certain setting, they would immediately seek his forgiveness. As we have noted before, a beautiful trait of the Prophet ﷺ was that he would rarely become angry and was always quick to forgive those who wronged him. All of this entails that it was very hard to make the Prophet ﷺ upset in the first place, since as ʿĀʾishah ﷺ related:

وَمَا انْتَقَمَ رَسُولُ اللهِ صَلَّى اللهُ عَلَيْهِ وَسَلَّم لِنَفْسِهِ فِي شَيْءٍ قَطُّ

"The Messenger of Allah ﷺ never got angry for himself."

At the same time, if one asked the Prophet ﷺ for forgiveness, he would always pardon them. This was regardless of how angry he was beforehand, and the gravity of the wrong in question.

The Prophet's beautiful characteristics relating to this theme are so numerous that they are hard to enumerate. Just one of these traits are worth discussing in further detail. The Prophet ﷺ did not allow a person's mistreatment or wrong towards him to overwhelm him. For example, 'Ā'ishah ﷺ describes how while being in charge of the city of Madinah, the Prophet ﷺ would sometimes be addressed with the pejorative phrase "al-sām 'alaykum", which means "death be upon you". These evildoers would quickly try to recite this phrase, so that it would be misheard as the typical greeting of "al-salām 'alaykum", which conveys the beautiful wish of peace for a person. They would recite it so quickly that it would be hard for an ordinary listener to realise they were being cursed, as the two words sounded similar. But eventually, the evil misdeeds of these people became evident. 'Ā'ishah ﷺ would not tolerate the usage of this profanity, and would respond with similar phrases, and asked that they be cursed or afflicted with death. In contrast, the Prophet ﷺ would ignore their statements, and take it as a simple matter. The Prophet ﷺ was the recognised leader of the city, but he never opted to escalate the issue. In fact, he would tell 'Ā'ishah to calm down and resist reciprocating such statements. 'Ā'ishah would say in response, "O Messenger of Allah! Did you not hear what they said?" But the Prophet ﷺ would extinguish her anger by saying: "And did you not hear what I responded with?

I said back to them 'and upon you (*wa 'alaykum*)'."
This was a beautiful and simple solution to the matter.
If they said *al-salām*, then they will be blessed with a
greeting in return. But if they said *al-sām*, then they
will receive the same profanity in return. He ﷺ then
reminded 'Āishah of his overarching philosophy in life
by stating: "O 'Āishah! Allah loves gentleness in all
His affairs." This moving story demonstrates that the
Prophet ﷺ would not allow the curses or profanities of
his opponents to cause him to reciprocate.

At the same time, the Prophet ﷺ never liked to hear
people discuss the faults and bad qualities found in
others. He also did not like people to convey negative
information regarding their fellow Muslims, as
this would lead to disruptions and schisms in the
community. He said in a beautiful hadith:

لَا يُبَلِّغُنِي أَحَدٌ مِنْ أَصْحَابِي عَنْ أَحَدٍ شَيْئًا، فَإِنِّي أُحِبُّ أَنْ أَخْرُجَ إِلَيْكُمْ
وَأَنَا سَلِيمُ الصَّدْرِ

"None of my Companions should convey to me
negative information about others, as I like to come
out to you while my heart is pure."

He ﷺ closed the door to gossiping and backbiting with
this statement, but even more importantly, he wanted
to close all the means of developing bad thoughts
towards any of his Companions. He ﷺ did not want to

have any dislike or enmity towards a fellow Muslim, which ultimately meant that he would not give this type of negative communication an audience. This type of description of him also appears in the Qur'an:

فَبِمَا رَحْمَةٍ مِنَ اللَّهِ لِنتَ لَهُمْ ۖ وَلَوْ كُنتَ فَظًّا غَلِيظَ الْقَلْبِ لَانفَضُّوا مِنْ حَوْلِكَ ۖ فَاعْفُ عَنْهُمْ وَاسْتَغْفِرْ لَهُمْ وَشَاوِرْهُمْ فِي الْأَمْرِ

"It is out of Allah's mercy that you have been lenient with them. Had you been cruel or hard-hearted, they would have certainly abandoned you. So pardon them, ask Allah's forgiveness for them, and consult with them in matters." [6]

This verse informs us that the Prophet ﷺ never had a negative and conflictual personality which repelled the people. The Companions who knew him at a close and personal level only confirmed his noble attributes. Anas ﷺ, for example, had a special vantage point, as he served the Prophet ﷺ for several years as a young boy. Despite this lengthy time serving him, he states: "The Prophet never used to say to me: 'Why did you do this?' or 'Why did you not do that?'" He also says:

كَانَ النَّبِيُّ صَلَّى اللَّهُ عَلَيْهِ وَسَلَّمَ أَحْسَنَ النَّاسِ خُلُقًا

"The Messenger of Allah ﷺ was the best of people in terms of character."

---

[6] *Āl ʿImrān*, 159.

Anas ※ illustrated this point by relating a moving
story: "When he once sent me to go run an errand, I
got caught up playing with the other children. When
the Prophet ※ found me, he simply smiled towards
me and asked: 'Anas, did you go where I instructed
you to?' I said: 'O Messenger, I am sorry. I will go
do it now.'" In another report, he said: "I served him
for nine years, but he never chastised me harshly on
anything, nor did he ask me: 'Why did you not do
this?' or 'Why did you did not do that?'" This was
the case, despite the fact that Anas was extremely
young and in a vulnerable position. Nevertheless, the
Prophet ※ was always gentle with him, and never took
a mistake or lapse as something serious. Instead, he ※
would always overlook a mistake and forgive him for
any oversights. He ※ would never chastise someone for
a slip, regardless of whether it was a family member or
a person who belonged to his community.

There were also more serious and life-threatening
situations which the Prophet ※ faced. There were
numerous individuals who sought to harm or take
the Prophet's life due to his call to Islam. As Anas ※
narrates, 80 men from Makkah launched an attack
and attempted to kill the Prophet ※; they were from
the people of al-Tanʿīm. These men had their full
body armour on, and intended to engage in battle.
The Prophet ※ was able to thwart their attack and

have them captured. The Prophet 攨 then simply let them go; he did not execute them or punish them in any way.

In fact, the Prophet 攨 did not just release his enemies physically by not holding them to account, but he also freed himself from any ill feelings or grudges. Take the case of Abū Ṭālib, who was not just an uncle, but a father figure for the Prophet. When Abū Ṭālib was on his deathbed, there were two individuals in the room who were exerting their best efforts to prevent Abū Ṭālib from saying *lā ilāha il Allāh* in his last moments. The first of these two individuals is well known among us: Abū Jahl. The second was ʿAbdullāh ibn Abī Umayyah 攨. Both of them would shout from the top of their lungs to prevent Abū Ṭālib from professing Islam. They would also say to Abū Ṭālib: "Are you on the religion of ʿAbd al-Muṭṭalib, or the religion of your son Muhammad?" Before his final breaths, Abū Ṭālib said, "I am on the religion of ʿAbd al-Muṭṭalib." Despite this sad and devastating chain of events, the Prophet 攨 forgave ʿAbdullāh ibn Abī Umayyah 攨, who later on became a Companion of the Prophet. In fact, the Prophet 攨 never reminded him of this incident related to Abū Ṭālib in the subsequent years that followed. As for Abū Jahl, it is well known that he died in a state of disbelief. But his son ʿIkrimah 攨 accepted Islam and became a

The Prophet ﷺ did not just release his enemies physically by not holding them to account, but he also freed himself from any ill feelings or grudges. When Abū Sufyān ﷺ admitted doing wrong, the Prophet ﷺ recited the response of Yūsuf ﷺ "There is no blame upon you today."

Companion of the Prophet ﷺ. The Prophet ﷺ used to order his other Companions to never mention Abū Jahl's name in front of him; mention of the label might hurt his feelings. By doing so, the Prophet ﷺ was taking into consideration the feelings that 'Ikrimah ؓ had for his father, despite the latter being one of the greatest enemies of Islam who persecuted the Prophet and caused Abū Ṭālib to die in a state of disbelief.

In a parallel manner, we come across the story of Hind, who ordered that Ḥamzah's liver be cut out, which she then chewed and spit out. After the Conquest of Makkah, she sought the Prophet's forgiveness, and the Prophet ﷺ fully pardoned her. Likewise, Waḥshī was also forgiven by the Prophet ﷺ, despite him being the person who carried out Hind's order by killing Ḥamzah.

Throughout the *sīrah* literature, we find numerous examples of the Prophet's forgiveness. In addition, upon examining these cases, we realise that the Prophet ﷺ often relied on the examples of his predecessors, just like how we rely on him. When Abū Sufyān said to the Prophet ﷺ, "We were wrong, and Allah has preferred you over us", the Prophet ﷺ recited the response of Yūsuf ؑ:

لَا تَثْرِيبَ عَلَيْكُمُ الْيَوْمَ

"There is no blame upon you today." [7]

Whenever he faced harm or difficulties from his
people, he would remind himself of the example of
Mūsā ﷺ: "May Allah have mercy upon my brother
Mūsā. He was hurt with much more than this, yet
he was still patient." As for the Prophet ﷺ, he had
one golden rule: if you sought his forgiveness for a
previous wrong, he ﷺ would fully pardon you and let
you begin with a fresh slate. It did not matter whether
this wrong was a misdemeanour or a gross injustice.
He ﷺ would move on and fully commit himself to
remembering his Lord during the night and seeking
His forgiveness.

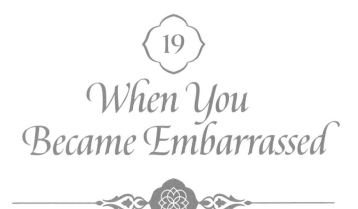

19

When You Became Embarrassed

The Prophet ﷺ was known to be a shepherd. He once said in a beautiful hadith that all prophets were shepherds at some point in their lives. And in order to effectively guide your flock, you must learn to be tolerant and patient. The Prophet ﷺ tolerated questions, even if they were posed in an inappropriate manner. During his life, young and inexperienced individuals would come to him and mention things in an awkward and unbecoming way. Despite these errors, the Prophet ﷺ would still encourage the people to come forth and ask their questions pertaining to the religion (dīn). That was so they may lift their state of ignorance and avoid falling into serious errors.

During the process of studying with the Prophet ﷺ or asking him questions, one finds numerous instances where people committed errors in his blessed presence.

When making mistakes in front of such a great man, it is easy for people to falsely believe that they have brought themselves to devastation and ruin. In numerous cases, we find Companions mentioning incidents where Bedouins would approach them and practise poor conduct in the presence of the Prophet ✿. Unlike town dwellers, Bedouins did not have refined manners, which meant that they would often address the Prophet ✿ in a loud and impolite tone, and even interrupt him during his sermon (*khuṭbah*) as well. They would also interrupt him in the middle of his teachings and conversations. At the same time, they would address him with an impolite and abrasive tone. In response to these types of interruptions, the Prophet ✿ would maintain his train of thought and continue his address. Stopping midway would deprive the entire gathering of his talk. Once he finished his lecture, he would then inquire who the questioner was, and address their concerns. This was the optimal way of keeping the audience engaged while also ensuring that the questioner's query was not squandered. For instance, there is the famous story of the man who addressed the Prophet ✿ during his sermon and asked: "When is the Hour?" The Prophet ✿ continued delivering his sermon, and upon finishing, he asked: "Where is the questioner?"

The Prophet ﷺ tolerated questions, even if they were posed in an inappropriate manner. Young and inexperienced individuals would mention things to him in an awkward and unbecoming way. The Prophet ﷺ would still encourage people to ask their questions so they may lift their state of ignorance and avoid falling into serious errors.

We also see the Prophet ﷺ in another hadith picking up dried nasal mucus found on the pulpit (*minbar*). He peeled it off himself, and asked: "Is there not a better place for people to leave this?" It is unbelievable that a person would actually dispose of this foul mucus on the Prophet's own pulpit, yet he ﷺ still exercised patience when this happened. On a similar note, we have the story where a man walked in the *masjid* while the Prophet was leading the Companions in prayer. This man had not become aware of the prohibition of speaking or giving greetings during the ritual prayer (*ṣalāh*). So upon entering, he issued the greeting of *al-salām ʿalaykum* to everyone, but he did not receive any response. Because his greetings were ignored, the man grew increasingly agitated and did not understand why everyone kept silent. He continued addressing the group of worshippers by saying: "What is wrong with you?" Despite his state of alarm, he still received no response. It was only after the prayer was concluded that the Prophet ﷺ addressed his concern. He addressed the congregation by saying: "Where is the person that asked the question as to why no one was responding to him?" The Prophet ﷺ entertained his question and validated his concerns. He stated that it used to be permissible to speak and issue greetings during the prayer in a moderate manner, just like in the case of circumambulation (*ṭawāf*). But now this concession had been abrogated.

And, of course, we are all aware of the famous story of the Bedouin who urinated in the Prophet's *masjid*. But before this incident occurred, the man felt unwelcome in the *masjid*, as his disheveled and unkempt appearance caused the Companions to become uneasy with him. After praying behind the Prophet ﷺ, he said in his *duʿāʾ*:

اللَّهُمَّ ارْحَمْنِي وَمُحَمَّدًا وَلَا تَرْحَمْ مَعَنَا أَحَدًا

"O Allah! Have mercy on me, and have mercy on Muhammad. But do not have mercy on anyone else."

The Prophet ﷺ turned towards him and said: "Indeed you have made that which is extremely expansive narrow and limited." The Prophet ﷺ was gently illustrating to him the point that Allah's mercy can encompass everyone. This is the background to the controversy that then followed. After this short conversation, the Bedouin proceeded towards the corner of the *masjid* and began urinating. While he was relieving himself, the Companions were shocked, and wanted to protect the sanctity of the Prophet's *masjid*. They immediately decided to stop him midway and then expel him from the place of prayer. However, the Prophet ﷺ ordered them to stop and told them to not startle the man. Instead, he ﷺ instructed them to wait until the Bedouin finished relieving himself. After he had completed the act, the

Prophet ﷺ ordered the Companions to take a bucket of water and pour it over the contaminated place. Then he turned to the Bedouin and said: "These *masjids* are places which have been made for the remembrance of Allah, and it is not befitting that a person urinate in them." Then the Prophet ﷺ directed his attention to the Companions, and told them the following golden words:

إِنَّمَا بُعِثْتُمْ مُيَسِّرِينَ وَلَمْ تُبْعَثُوا مُعَسِّرِينَ

"You were sent to bring ease to the people, and you were not sent to bring hardship."

Since we find ourselves in the month of Ramadan, it is most appropriate to mention the beautiful story of Salamah ibn Sakhr ﷺ, who was a young Companion that had a very strong sexual appetite. In fact, he said:

كُنْتُ امْرَأً أُصِيبُ مِن النِّسَاءِ مَا لَا يُصِيبُ غَيْرِي

"I was a person who would engage in sexual intercourse with women far more than anyone else could."

Because of his uncontrollable sexual desire, he believed it was necessary that he do something which could curb his intimacy. He actually prohibited himself from engaging in intercourse with his wife by announcing a prohibited form of divorce upon her, which is known as *ẓihār*. This was a common form of divorce in pre-Islamic times, where someone pronounces that their wife is like their mother's back. The ruling and expiation for this form of divorce is discussed in *Surah al-Mujādilah*. Despite his commitment to leave all forms of sexual intimacy, it did not take long for Salamah to resume back to the previous state of affairs. He mentioned that one night, he saw a part of his wife's legs, and he could not hold himself any longer (*lam albath an nazawtu ʿalayhā*). It is self-evident what happened next: he became sexually intimate with her.

The next morning he went to his people and informed them of what happened. They suggested to him that he was now in a serious predicament, and would have no way of avoiding the consequences. Salamah ﷺ suggested some members of his people accompany him towards the Messenger of Allah ﷺ, but they said: "No, by Allah." Salamah said: "So I went to the Messenger of Allah ﷺ and informed him of happened. The Prophet ﷺ said: 'Did you really do that (*anta bi dhāk*), O Salamah?' I said: 'Twice, O Messenger of Allah. I am content with the judgement of Allah, so you may rule against me as you wish.'" Here, Salamah indicated to the Prophet ﷺ that he would fully submit to the judgement decreed by Allah.

*W*hen people went to
the Prophet ﷺ after having
committed an error or misdeed,
he ﷺ would not warn them of
their doom or fail to help them.
Instead, he would search for
a feasible solution, put them
at ease and direct them to
a realistic and appropriate
course of action so they
would return to Allah and
trek the right path.

So the Prophet ﷺ said that he should free a slave. Salamah said in response: "By the One Who sent you with the truth, I do not own a neck besides this one." And he struck the surface of his own neck to indicate that he could not free anyone else's neck, since this was the only neck he had. So the Prophet ﷺ said: "Then fast two consecutive months." Salamah said in response: "What happened was actually a result of me fasting in the first place." At first, Salamah said that he would submit to any decision delivered by the Prophet ﷺ, but now he was making excuses once the Prophet ﷺ made prescriptions. Then the Prophet ﷺ said: "Feed sixty people with a *wasaq* of dried dates." Salamah said: "By the One Who sent you with the truth, we are the hungriest of people. We pass nights without having any food in our house." So the Prophet ﷺ went inside and brought him a basket of dates. He then provided Salamah the following instructions: "Go out and feed sixty people, and then afterwards feed yourself and your family with any amount left over."

So Salamah ﷺ returned back to his people. Instead of being destroyed or devastated as everyone expected his fate to be, he was blessed with this food. It was given to him by the Prophet ﷺ himself, and it would now be distributed amongst everyone. He then addressed his people by saying:

وَجَدْتُ عِنْدَكُمُ الضِّيقَ وَسُوءَ الرَّأْيِ وَوَجَدْتُ عِنْدَ النَّبِيِّ صَلَّى اللَّهُ عَلَيْهِ
وَسَلَّمَ السَّعَةَ وَحُسْنَ الرَّأْيِ

"With you I only found doom and bad thoughts,
but with the Prophet I found expansiveness and
a good opinion."

This is what people consistently found with the
Prophet ﷺ. When they went to him after having
committed an error or misdeed, he ﷺ would not warn
them of their doom or fail to help them. Instead, he
would always search for a feasible solution and put
them at ease. In addition, he would direct them to
a realistic and appropriate course of action so they
would return to Allah and trek the right path.

When You Noticed His Poverty

There is no doubt that one of the strongest proofs of the Messenger's claim to prophethood was his eminent character. He ﷺ was endowed with the best manners (*akhlāq*) imaginable. If you saw him, you would be struck by his sincerity towards Allah and His creation, and would have no doubts that he ﷺ is indeed a Prophet. Furthermore, if you think back to the Makkan stage, you will recall that the polytheists exerted their greatest efforts to strike a compromise with the Prophet ﷺ. They were trying to scrutinise him and identify whether he ﷺ was making this new call for some ulterior motive, which is why they offered him wealth, power, and gifts. Their approach with the Prophet ﷺ is encapsulated in the following verse:

وَدُّواْ لَوْ تُدْهِنُ فَيُدْهِنُونَ

*"They wish you would compromise so they
would yield."* [8]

Yet, the Prophet ﷺ rejected all their offers and opted
to endure their persecution. This was completely
shocking for the polytheists, since they were morally
bankrupt people. When he ﷺ was in Madinah, no
one would bat an eyelid if he lived a decent life. But
in Makkah, the Prophet ﷺ was living in absolute
poverty, a state which everyone was witnessing. In
fact, his state was far worse than how it may have
appeared to the public eye.

Had he wanted, the Prophet ﷺ could have become one
of the richest people in history. Had he indicated his
desire, the wealthy Companions like 'Abd al-Raḥmān
ibn 'Awf, 'Uthmān, and Ṭalḥah ﷺ would have ensured
he ﷺ had as many palaces as he wanted. In fact,
many Companions felt that as a leader and Prophet,
he ﷺ deserved to live a comfortable and affluent life.
But the Prophet ﷺ chose to always live an extremely
humble life. Because of his generosity and openness
to others, it was easy to miss just how much hunger
the Prophet ﷺ experienced, and how much he
suffered due to poverty. On this matter, Anas ibn

---

[8] *al-Qalam*, 9.

Mālik ﷺ said: "Not once did the Prophet ﷺ have food for the next day." This means that the Prophet ﷺ lived his life on a day-to-day basis, without having any stable state of living.

The only person who recognised his dire state of hunger on a given night was none other than Abū Bakr ﷺ, who was also suffering from starvation. The Prophet ﷺ once went outside in the middle of the night, and he coincidently crossed paths with Abū Bakr ﷺ. It did not take long for them to realise that both of them were outside for the same reason: to look for food. Just reflect on this story for a moment: how could the best of creation and the most beloved member of society suffer this much from hunger? Nobody had realised that he ﷺ was so hungry that he was forced to go outside in order to find a few morsels and ensure his survival.

Once one scans the *sīrah* literature, they will come to the conclusion that during difficult times, the Prophet ﷺ would always suffer more than anyone else. We have already discussed a moving story which occurred during the Battle of the Trench (*al-Khandaq*), where Jābir witnessed how bloated the Prophet's stomach was out of hunger. It was most obvious that the Prophet ﷺ had not eaten anything for several days. Furthermore, in another report, Abū Ṭalḥah ﷺ said to Umm Sulaym ﷺ: "I heard the voice of the

Messenger of Allah ﷺ, where one could detect the hunger in his voice." Try to simply imagine how severe the Prophet's state must have been if people could discern his hunger through his voice. He then asked Umm Sulaym if she had anything that could be served to the Prophet ﷺ. Umm Sulaym said that food was available for the Messenger of Allah ﷺ by all means. In another report, Anas ؓ interestingly stated that the Prophet ﷺ would sometimes reflect on his state of hunger and how it affected him. If you saw him suffering from hunger and assumed that it was his worst day, he ﷺ would actually correct you and mention other days which were far worse. He also stated that the Prophet ﷺ mentioned his hardest life moment; this was an episode where he had to bear hunger for 30 days and nights. During this state, he ﷺ had to spend those days alone with Bilāl ؓ, where the two could not find anything that was suitable for consumption, save for a small amount of food that was hidden under the armpit of Bilāl ؓ. Just try to imagine how difficult it was for both of them to bear an entire month without any suitable food to eat, except for a few crumbs that they could salvage.

It is thus no surprise to find the famous incident when ʿUmar ؓ entered upon the Prophet ﷺ and witnessed firsthand the difficult circumstances that the Prophet ﷺ had to withstand on a daily basis. In this hadith,

The Prophet ﷺ wanted to stress the point that we should be pleased with the eternal riches and wealth in the Hereafter over the transient goods of this world, which merely distract us and cause us to turn away from what is of true value. We are a nation which examines things from an other-worldly perspective.

'Umar ﷺ provides a detailed description of the Prophet's simple living conditions. He mentioned that the Prophet ﷺ would rest and sleep on a simple and rough rug (*ḥaṣīr*). The Prophet ﷺ did not have any furniture in his house, so would use this rug as a mattress to sleep on during the night, and would also rest on it during the day by folding it up. If someone visited the Prophet ﷺ, he would allow the guest to sit on the rug. He ﷺ would then place a cushion between himself and the visitor. One may then say that this rug also functioned as a form of household furniture.

When 'Umar ﷺ entered the Prophet's room, he saw him lying directly on the rug. The Prophet ﷺ had nothing to protect his body from the coarse composition of the rug, save his waist-wrap. Since the rug was made of tree branches, it was very stiff and rough. When the Prophet ﷺ rose up from the rug, 'Umar ﷺ noticed that the marks of the branches could be found on his body. This reveals that it must been extremely painful to rest or sleep on this rug. When 'Umar ﷺ scanned the rest of the space, he found nothing except a handful of barley and a few leaves on the corner of the room. The only other thing he could find was a waterskin hung up on his room, which barely contained any water. After witnessing this saddening sight, 'Umar ﷺ could not control himself, and began to weep profusely. The Prophet ﷺ said in response:

مَا يُبْكِيكَ يَا ابْنَ الْخَطَّابِ

"What makes you weep, O Ibn al-Khaṭṭab?"

'Umar ﷺ said: "O Messenger of Allah! How can I not weep when I see this rug has bruised your body, and I do not see anything in your room save these few things? This is while Khosrow (Kisrā) and Caesar live amongst rivers and gardens. But you are the Prophet of Allah and His chosen one, while this is all that you have in your room?" The Prophet ﷺ said in response:

يَا بْنَ الْخَطَّابِ أَمَا تَرْضَى أَنْ تَكُونَ لَنَا الْآخِرَةُ وَلَهُم الدُّنيا

"O Ibn al-Khaṭṭab, are you not pleased to know that the Hereafter is ours while the world is theirs?"

The Prophet did not want 'Umar ﷺ to leave his room without imparting a priceless lesson for the *ummah*. He wanted to stress the point that the Hereafter belongs to us, and we are a nation which examines things from an other-worldly perspective. We pursue the eternal riches and wealth that is found in the Hereafter, not the transient goods of this world, which merely distract us and cause us to turn away from what is of true value. In essence, the Prophet ﷺ was telling 'Umar ﷺ that he should be pleased that we have the Hereafter, and be content with others possessing this world.

The next time you have a feeling of entitlement and craving for more, I want you to remember this powerful narration from ʿĀʾishah ﷺ. It is mentioned that she would never eat a full meal except that she would start to cry. The people around her would ask, "Why are you crying, O Mother of the Believers?" She said in response:

مَا أَشْبَعُ مِنْ طَعَامٍ إِلَّا وَأَبْكِى لِأَنِّي أَذْكُرَ الْحَالَ الَّتِى فَارَقَ عَلَيْهَا رَسُولُ اللهِ صَلَّى اللهُ عَلَيْهِ وَسَلَّمَ الدُّنْيَا

"I do not satiate myself with any food except that
I start to cry because I remember the way that the
Prophet ﷺ left this world."

She ﷺ also said:

وَاللهِ مَا شَبِعَ مِنْ خُبْزٍ وَلَحْمٍ مَرَّتَيْنِ فِي الْيَوْم

"I swear by Allah that he never ate to his fill of bread
or meat twice in a day."

Through these accounts, ʿĀʾishah ﷺ was remembering the difficulties that the Prophet ﷺ experienced during his life. Regardless of whether one has lived in the past or in the present, they must always curb their perception of entitlement to this world by recalling how Allah's most beloved person experienced severe poverty. In fact, poverty was actually the least of his difficulties and hardships.

When He Lost His Child

It was one thing to witness the Prophet ﷺ suffer from hunger and poverty. But it was even more discomforting to see him undergo the emotional grief and pain that a human experiences when they lose a loved one. For his followers, the Prophet ﷺ enjoyed a special rank; he was their superman. Here we should draw a distinction between the natural tears he displayed when remembering Allah in ritual prayer (ṣalāh), as opposed to the severe grief he experienced after he witnessed a tragedy occur in his household. It was extremely uncomfortable to see the Prophet ﷺ in this latter state.

The Prophet ﷺ had to bury six out of the seven children he had in this world, which meant he faced tragedy in several chapters of his life. We usually mention all these deaths in a generic way, where all

the names of the deceased children are clustered
together. While it is true that the death of every child
gave him immense heartbreak, the death of Ibrāhīm
was particularly tragic due to its unique timing and
context. First and foremost, Ibrāhīm was born when
the Prophet ✺ was 62 years of age, which implies that
he was born when the Prophet ✺ was nearing the end
of his life. Secondly, Ibrāhīm's birth came more than
20 years after the birth of the Prophet's previous child,
Fāṭimah ✺. Before Ibrāhīm's arrival, Fāṭimah ✺ was
the only surviving child of the Prophet ✺, as all the
five other children that the Prophet ✺ had with his
first wife Khadījah ✺ had passed away. His two sons
died during their childhood. His three other daughters
lived up to adulthood, but they died shortly after
being married or having children. This meant that
the Prophet had to witness the burial of almost all
his offspring. Fāṭimah ✺ was at this point a married
woman, and had children of her own. The Prophet ✺
considered Fāṭimah's children to be like his own.

But now, just as his life was nearing its end, the
Prophet ✺ was blessed with the greatest thing
possible: his own son. There was much joy tied
with the birth of this baby boy. What made Ibrāhīm
extremely special was that he was the only son that
the Prophet ✺ had since the beginning of the Islamic
message and his prophetic mission. The Prophet ✺

was thus able to give his son Ibrāhīm all the Islamic rituals, just like how he performed them for the children of other Companions. This included reading the call of prayer (adhān) in his ear, performing the tahnīk by rubbing a chewed date up the newborn's palate, and offering the 'aqīqah sacrifice. With immense pride and joy, the Prophet ﷺ performed these rituals. He then held up his baby boy and addressed the people by saying:

لَقَدْ رَزَقَ اللهُ نَبِيَّكُمْ وَلَدًا وَسَمَّيْتُهُ عَلَى أَبِى إِبْرَاهِيمَ

"Look O people! Allah has blessed your Prophet with a son, and I have named him after my father Ibrāhīm."

Subḥānallāh, what a scene this must have been! Imagine being inside the *masjid* and having the opportunity to see the Prophet ﷺ hold Ibrāhīm for the first time, while also witnessing the 'aqīqah ritual. It is most evident that the Prophet ﷺ had an intimate attachment to this baby, as he was known to visit the newborn on a daily basis when it was under the care of its wet nurse. The Prophet ﷺ would bring his baby with him whenever he went to visit the homes of his spouses. And of course, he would take Ibrāhīm to the *masjid* as well. Through these various actions it is evident that the Prophet ﷺ was exceptionally excited with his newborn son. After all these years of grief

Before Ibrāhīm's arrival, Fāṭimah ﷺ was the only surviving child of the Prophet ﷺ, as all the five other children that he ﷺ had with his first wife Khadījah ﷺ had passed away. This meant that the Prophet ﷺ had to witness the burial of almost all his offspring during his lifetime.

and tragedy, it appeared that he would finally have
a son who would survive him after his death and
preserve his blood line.

But these expectations unfortunately did not
materialise, as things deteriorated very quickly when
Ibrāhīm was 16 months old. What makes this episode
even more saddening was that at the age of 16 months,
a baby develops a personality and forms strong
connections with a parent. It was tragic then to know
that these connections would not last anymore in this
world. Anas ibn Mālik ﷺ narrates in detail how the
Prophet ﷺ exited from the home of the wet nurse on
that fateful day. The Prophet ﷺ was informed earlier
that day that Ibrāhīm had become really sick, and all
indicators pointed to the conclusion that he would
die soon. The Prophet left what he was doing, and
immediately headed towards the residence of the wet
nurse with some of his Companions. The husband of
the wet nurse was known by the name of Abū Sayf,
who worked as a blacksmith. The Prophet ﷺ requested
his permission to enter his house in order to see
Ibrāhīm. After being granted the man's approval, the
Prophet ﷺ entered the house to take his son. This was
an intensely emotional moment, as the Prophet ﷺ was
a proud father who intensely loved this baby, but was
now watching it die before his eyes. He took Ibrāhīm
in his arms, held him tightly, kissed him, and started

smelling his hair. The Companions quietly watched the Prophet in this tearful scene. It was difficult for them to witness their Prophet in this grief, as he was situated in a purely human and vulnerable moment. As time passed, Ibrāhīm started to breathe with more difficulty, and at a slower pace. Anas ✾ then said that Ibrāhīm was in the arms of the Prophet ✾ when his soul left his body. Just imagine how difficult it must be for a father to have their own child breathe their last while they are in their arms. Now imagine this happening with the Prophet ✾, who was known for having a blessed heart brimming with love and mercy.

Shortly after the death of his son, the Prophet ✾ began to weep. Upon seeing this sight, ʿAbd al-Raḥmān ibn ʿAwf ✾ asked in surprise, "You too, O Messenger of Allah?" He was not asking this question out of cruelty or malice. This was completely different from the case of the man who arrogantly asked the Prophet ✾ why he gave his grandsons al-Ḥasan and al-Ḥusayn ✾ so much affection. Instead, ʿAbd al-Raḥmān ibn ʿAwf's question was asked out of admiration towards the Prophet ✾, as in to say: "You cry as well, just like us?" They were not used to seeing the Prophet ✾ break down like this, even if in this scenario his intense grief pertained to the death of his child. This type of intense weeping was only observed in other people, not a person of the stature and eminence like the Prophet ✾.

When the Prophet ﷺ wept following the death of his son Ibrahim in his arms, he ﷺ explained that his emotional response was a form of mercy that Allah ﷻ put in the soul; his tears were a form of divine mercy that Allah ﷻ inspired in his heart. In other words, this type of emotional response was beyond his control.

In response, the Prophet ﷺ looked at ʿAbd al-Raḥmān ibn ʿAwf ﷺ and said:

يَا ابْنَ عَوْفٍ إِنَّهَا رَحْمَةٌ

"O Ibn ʿAwf, this is a mercy."

By this statement, the Prophet ﷺ meant that his emotional response was a form of mercy that Allah ﷻ put in the soul; his tears were a form of divine mercy that Allah ﷻ inspired in his heart. In other words, this type of emotional response was beyond his control. He could not help himself but cry, as he immensely loved his child and had to mourn his loss. Anas ﷺ then stated that the Prophet ﷺ started to weep even more. Upon seeing this sight, the Companions began to cry as well. How could they not, when the Prophet ﷺ was holding his dead son at that point? Then the Prophet ﷺ said:

إِنَّ الْعَيْنَ تَدْمَعُ، وَالْقَلْبَ يَحْزَنُ، وَلاَ نَقُولُ إِلَّا مَا يُرْضِي رَبَّنَا، وَإِنَّا بِفِرَاقِكَ يَا إِبْرَاهِيمُ لَمَحْزُونُونَ

"The eyes shed tears, the heart feels sadness, but we do not say anything except that which is pleasing to Allah. We are immensely saddened over your departure, O Ibrāhīm."

The Prophet had the pleasure of celebrating the birth of his son, who was the only boy he had since the beginning of the Islamic mission. He was able to perform all of the required and voluntary rituals for him. But now, it very soon came to an end. He had to go through the pain of performing the necessary funeral (*janāzah*) rituals over this baby which he loved so much. He had to wash and shroud Ibrāhīm's body, and then lead the funeral prayer over him. Then he had to carry his deceased body to its resting place, and have it covered with dirt.

Anyone who lived in Madinah on that day would have seen an amazing but frightening spectacle: a solar eclipse. What made this event more shocking was that it occurred on the same day of Ibrāhīm's death. If you were a Companion living in the city that day, you may have been shocked by this event, and probably would have drawn a connection between the two spectacular matters. In fact, you might believe that this was the case, as the Prophet's grief was extreme and unprecedented. Several Companions concluded that the sun was eclipsed due to the death of Ibrāhīm; surely this could not be a coincidence.

The Prophet came out and proceeded to lead the eclipse prayer (*ṣalāh al-kusūf*). His prayer was so lengthy that it would likely make someone behind him faint. He was praying for Allah's mercy during the time of this frightening eclipse. One could imagine the grief and hardship that he was facing that day, but he did not allow those emotions to prevent him from teaching the Companions the rituals they should perform when natural phenomena like this occur. He was a teacher *par excellence*; his heart was softened and bleeding due to his loss, but he always remembered and thanked his Lord. He never said anything which displeased his Lord. Through his actions that day, he was indirectly teaching us how we should grieve, and why we must always turn back to Allah ﷻ.

After concluding the prayer, the Prophet turned to the people and said: "The sun and the moon are from among the signs (*āyāt*) of Allah. They are not eclipsed due to the death or birth of anyone. So when you see them occur, then make *duʿāʾ*, pray, and give charity."

Even during this difficult tragedy he was facing, the Prophet was teaching his *ummah* through his actions and words. If you ever feel pain, remember that your Prophet felt greater pain. If you cry, remember how much your Prophet wept when he lost his beloved son at the end of his life. But most importantly, always remember how the Prophet exercised patience and gratitude. Despite his immense loss that day, the only thing that could be heard from him was *Alḥamdulillah*, since his heart was only full of thankfulness.

22

When He
Received Revelation

None of us were present with the Prophet ﷺ on the suspenseful Night of Power (*laylah al-qadr*), which was the first time he received revelation. Instead, the Prophet ﷺ was all alone when he met Jibrīl ﷺ for the first time and received Allah's divine revelation. It was evident from the first squeeze that he ﷺ received from Jibrīl ﷺ that this would be a momentous and difficult undertaking. In fact, Allah ﷻ says in the Qur'an:

إِنَّا سَنُلْقِى عَلَيْكَ قَوْلًا ثَقِيلًا

"We will soon send upon you a weighty revelation." [9]

Even though no one witnessed the first portion of revelation, an inhabitant of the city of Madinah was likely to see later parts of the Qur'an be revealed to

---

[9] *al-Muzzammil*, 5.

the Prophet ✿. Anyone who had the chance to see this unique event occur live in front of them affirmed that it was a spectacular sight.

Despite its metaphysical nature, the revelation would have its severe toll on the Prophet ✿, and press down upon him like a heavy weight. Regarding the sheer power of the revelation, Ibn Mas'ūd relates the following hadith from the Prophet ✿: "When Allah speaks to send the revelation, the inhabitants of the heavens hear the clinging of a bell from the other heaven above it. And it is like pulling a chain from Mount Ṣafā."

The sound of the revelation is so powerful that it even causes the angels (malā'ikah) to faint. And as Jibrīl ✿ comes by, they ask him: "O Jibrīl! What did your Lord say? What did your Lord say?" Jibrīl says in response:

الحَقُّ، الحَقُّ، وَهُوَ العَلِيُّ الكَبِيرُ

"He spoke the truth, He spoke the truth. And He is the Most High, the Most Great."

Reflect on this report for a moment; when Jibrīl ✿ received the revelation its sound caused other angels to faint due to its intense power. This revelation would then be brought down to the Prophet ✿, where he would receive Allah's words in front of the eyes of his Companions.

'Abdullāh ibn 'Abbās relates: "I remember when *Surah al-Anʿā*m was revealed to the Prophet ﷺ. He looked up to the sky, as Jibrīl ﷺ was descending towards him with the company of 70,000 angels, which were all escorting *Surah al-Anʿām*. They were praising Allah as it was coming down to the Prophet ﷺ. And the Prophet ﷺ looked up, and observed how the horizons were covered as it was approaching him. During this incident, he was sitting on a camel. Once the revelation reached him, the knees of the camel started to buckle because of the heavy toll that was being exerted upon the Prophet ﷺ." *Surah al-Anʿām* is more than 20 pages long, and all of it was revealed to the Prophet ﷺ at once. Add to this how the chapter came to him with this grand reception and majesty; it cannot even be imagined how strong of an impact these episodes of revelation must have had on the Prophet's heart. Regarding the immense power and impact of the Qur'an, Allah ﷻ says:

لَوْ أَنزَلْنَا هَذَا الْقُرْآنَ عَلَى جَبَلٍ لَّرَأَيْتَهُ خَاشِعًا مُّتَصَدِّعًا مِّنْ خَشْيَةِ اللهِ

"If we had sent down this Qur'an upon a mountain you would have seen it humbled and coming apart from the awe of Allah."[10]

---

[10] *al-Hashr*, 21.

The Companions were aware of this verse, and could only wonder how much of an impact the Qur'an must have had on the Prophet's soul and body. They wanted to know how the Prophet ✾ felt whenever the revelation descended upon him. In response to this question, the Prophet ✾ mentioned that it was the most difficult to receive when it came in one particular form, that is, where it sounded like the ringing of a heavy bell (ṣalṣalah al-jaras). The Prophet ✾ would focus carefully while receiving the divine words from Jibrīl ✾, lest he forgot any of the words he heard. 'Ā'ishah ✾ mentions that the descent of the Qur'an would seriously affect the Prophet ✾, as he would perspire profusely; beads of sweat would develop on his face, even when the weather was cold. He would also intensely shiver, as the divine words would seize his entire body. However, it is important to note that the Prophet ✾ would leave this state almost immediately once the transfer of revelation was complete. Without any pause or struggle, the Prophet ✾ would be able to smoothly and perfectly recite the portion of revelation. Once it had settled in his heart, all this revelation would be articulated afterwards by the Prophet ✾ with the greatest ease.

The Qur'an would settle deeply in the heart of the Prophet ﷺ, with the permission of Allah. He would then recite it to his Companions, and his scribes would write the revealed verses down. Zayd ibn Thābit رضي الله عنه was one of the most prominent scribes of the Qur'an.

Regarding this matter, Allah says:

لَا تُحَرِّكْ بِهِ لِسَانَكَ لِتَعْجَلَ بِهِ إِنَّ عَلَيْنَا جَمْعَهُ وَقُرْآنَهُ

*"Do not rush your tongue trying to memorise the
Quran. It is certainly upon Us to memorise and
recite it."*[11]

The Qur'an would accordingly settle deeply in the
heart of the Prophet ✿, with the permission of Allah.
He would then recite it to his Companions, and his
scribes would write the revealed verses down. Zayd ibn
Thābit ✿ was one of the most prominent scribes of
the Qur'an. He noted that the moment the Prophet ✿
began to recite a new portion of revelation, he would
begin writing it down. He said: "There was one
occasion where the revelation (*waḥy*) came down,
and the Prophet's leg happened to be resting on mine.
The Prophet's body became heavy to the extent that
I thought my leg had broken, and that I would never
have the ability to walk afterwards." Despite the
pressure and stress that came from the revelation,
the Prophet ✿ carried that weight on a regular basis
for his *ummah*. The Companions would witness this
firsthand, and attested to how much discomfort the
Prophet ✿ underwent in this process. In fact, there
are several narrations which indicate how the riding

---

[11] *al-Qiyāmah*, 16.

animals of the Prophet ﷺ would struggle immensely while carrying him when revelation descended.

But what did this acquirement of revelation look like, and what would one hear from the Prophet when this process was occurring? ʿUmar ibn al-Khaṭṭāb ﷺ has answered both questions for us through his vivid account of how the Prophet ﷺ received Allah's divine words. He mentioned that it was clear whenever the Prophet ﷺ was in the midst of receiving the Qurʾan from Jibrīl ﷺ, because it was a state unlike any other. One could also hear a sound around him, which resembled the humming of bees. It was clear that some words were being recited and transferred to the Prophet ﷺ. As difficult as it was on the Prophet's body, the words around his head were soft and melodious. On one day, ʿUmar ﷺ mentioned that the revelation came down to the Prophet ﷺ, and after receiving it, he paused and raised his hands towards the prayer direction (*qiblah*). He ﷺ then made a beautiful and amazing *duʿāʾ* which everyone should memorise and recite regularly:

اللَّهُمَ زِدْنَا وَلَا تُنْقِصْنَا، وَأَكْرِمْنَا وَلَا تُهِنَّا، وَأَعْطِنَا وَلَا تَحْرِمْنَا، وَآثِرْنَا وَلَا تُؤْثِرْ عَلَيْنَا، وَأَرْضِنَا وَارْضَ عَنَّا

"O Allah, give us more and not less, honour us and do not disgrace us, give us and do not withhold from us, choose us and do not choose others over us, and please us and be pleased with us."

This is an amazing supplication which the Prophet ☙ made immediately after receiving a passage from the Qur'an. When he asked to be given more, he was referring to revelation. 'Umar ibn al-Khaṭṭāb ☙ then mentioned that after finishing his prayer, he ☙ turned around to them and said: "Allah has sent me ten verses. Whoever acts upon these verses will enter Paradise:

قَدْ أَفْلَحَ الْمُؤْمِنُون

'Successful indeed are the believers...'"[12]

He recited the first 10 verses of *Surah al-Mu'minūn*. Thus, we observe that the Prophet ☙ would always be grateful for the powerful revelation he received on a regular basis, and would accordingly respond with these powerful and beautiful supplications. In fact, he would become pleased when his allotted portion of revelation increased, as that only further elevated his status and secured his path to Paradise (*Jannah*).

---

[12] *al-Mu'minūn*, 1-10.

When He
Performed Miracles

While it is true that the original descent of revelation to the Prophet ﷺ was a unique and powerful sight, the Qur'an is just as miraculous and majestic as it was then. While we never saw the Prophet ﷺ or his experience with revelation directly like the Companions did, we still nevertheless can directly read and experience the power of the words which were revealed to him. This is because the miraculous nature of the Qur'an is timeless and permanent. But the Qur'an was not the only miracle; the Prophet ﷺ performed a number of amazing feats which demonstrated the truth of his message. What was it like to directly witness the Prophet ﷺ perform these miracles? And was there a benefit or wisdom behind these miracles, as they unfolded in front of the eyes of the people?

I would like to focus on two different categories of miracles which the Prophet ※ would perform in front of the people in a regular basis. The first was how different beings of nature, such as rocks and trees, would both adore and greet him. It was astonishingly beautiful that even nature had an attachment with him. Related to this point, remember how the Prophet ※ mentioned that the student of sacred knowledge receives *du'ā'* from everyone and everything in the world. This *ipso facto* includes everything in the environment, such as the animals on the ground and the fish in the sea. The reason for why this is the case is obvious: the student of knowledge benefits everyone and everything around them. Of course, the Prophet ※ was the most blessed of those who were given knowledge, since he received divine revelation directly from the heavens.

Even before directly receiving revelation, the Prophet ※ would have these types of miracles occur with him while he was growing up. Nature had an intimate connection with him throughout his life. For instance, the trees would extend their branches towards him, and the stones would give him greetings (*salām*). But the Prophet ※ would for the most part ignore these phenomena, as he did not know what significance they held in this early stage of his life. But after reaching the age of 40 and being blessed with Prophethood, everything now became clear. Jābir ibn Samurah ※

relates the following report from the Prophet ﷺ after
he received revelation and became a Messenger of
Allah: "I recognise the stone in Makkah which used
to give me the greeting before my advent as a Prophet.
I still recognise that stone in the present moment."
Likewise, ʿAlī ibn Abī Ṭālib ﷺ related the following
report: "When we would go out in Makkah even
during the early days of the Prophet's divine mission,
the trees and rocks that we would pass would address
him by saying, 'Peace be upon you, O Messenger
of Allah!'" In another report, Anas ibn Mālik ﷺ
says: "Once we were with the Messenger of Allah ﷺ
and he had a small number of stones in his hand.
While they were in his palm, they would constantly
do *tasbīḥ*." It is remarkable that they would audibly
praise and remember Allah while being in the hand
of the Prophet ﷺ. Ultimately, it was common to find
elements of nature showering blessings upon the
Prophet ﷺ, because they felt blessed by his presence.

The most well-known story in this regard was
witnessed and related by numerous Companions. It is
a very moving scene, and I would like you to imagine
what follows. Initially, when delivering the Friday
sermon (*khuṭbah*), the Prophet ﷺ would stand by and
lean on a tree when speaking. Then, on a particular
week, a woman from the Helpers said to the Prophet:
"O Messenger of Allah, should we make a pulpit

*N*ature had an intimate connection with the Prophet ﷺ. The trees would extend their branches towards him, and the stones would greet him. The student of sacred knowledge receives du'ā' from everyone and everything in the world. He was of course, the most blessed of them as he received divine revelation directly from the heavens.

(*minbar*) for you?" The Prophet ﷺ said in response to her proposal:

$$إِنْ شِئْتُم$$

"If you wish [then go ahead and do so]."

So they built him a pulpit, and from that moment onwards the Prophet ﷺ decided to give his weekly sermon from it every Friday. But they noted that when the Prophet ﷺ began doing this, the date-palm tree started to cry like a child. Other Companions described the tree's weeping as being like a pregnant she-camel about to give birth. Can you imagine sitting there and witnessing such a scene? How would you react if you saw a tree crying in front of you like a baby or animal?

What the Prophet ﷺ did next was absolutely incredible and reveals the level of his mercy. He ﷺ descended from his pulpit and then approached the tree. He ﷺ began comforting the tree with his blessed presence. He ﷺ displayed gentleness and tenderness towards it, just like how a parent consoles a distressed child. While the Prophet was doing this, all of the Companions were staring in disbelief, and were likely asking themselves whether what was unfolding before their eyes was true. What an amazing moment this must have been. The Prophet ﷺ then explained to the Companions what had happened:

كَانَتْ تَبْكِي عَلَى مَا كَانَتْ تَسْمَعُ مِنَ الذِّكْرِ عِنْدَهَا

"It is crying because it is missing the words of remembrance it used to hear."

Because the Prophet ﷺ had moved to the pulpit, the tree was saddened since the Prophet ﷺ would no longer lean upon it and speak near its presence. This is the first category of miracles which was associated with the Prophet ﷺ. For the last example, undoubtedly numerous Companions would have seen it, since it occurred during the Friday prayer.

In addition, there was another category of miracles, which related to the abundant blessings that his hands produced and brought forth. By touching something, he ﷺ was able to produce one of two things: cause something unproductive to become fruitful, or exponentially increase the small quantity of a good or substance. For the former case, we have narrations where the Prophet ﷺ would touch the udders of cattle which were dried up. But after making contact with them, they began to flow with milk. An example of this can be found in the story of Umm Maʿbad ؆, where the Prophet ﷺ made her sick goat healthy and had it replenished with milk. In the latter case, there are numerous narrations where the Prophet ﷺ caused small quantities of food or water to become plentiful simply by making contact with them. ʿAbd al-Raḥmān

The Prophet ﷺ was exhibiting mercy (raḥmah) through the many miracles he received. That is because through his love and kindness, the Prophet ﷺ always gives members of his ummah more than what they initially expect, whether in this world or the Hereafter.

ibn Abī Bakr ✿ narrates in a noteworthy narration
that there were about 130 people who had gathered
with the Prophet ✿. The Prophet ✿ asked: "Do any
of you have any food with you?" Every one of the
attendees had brought a small amount of food, with
the total sum ultimately being mixed together. The
Prophet ✿ noticed that there was a man who owned
a flock of sheep, so he addressed him by stating:
"Are you selling these sheep? Or are you giving them
away?" The man replied by stating that he was only
selling them. As a result, the Prophet ✿ bought one
of these sheep. ʿAbd al-Raḥmān ✿ added that the
Prophet ✿ cooked the sheep all by himself, and upon
preparing it, began to cut and divide it into portions.
Then he proceeded to serve the people from it. From
his own blessed hand, he served all the 130 attendees
from this one sheep. Every person was given a portion
of food. In fact, ʿAbd al-Raḥmān ✿ even noted: "We
were able to put away some of the extra food for
our families." This story reveals how the Prophet ✿
was able to double the number of servings from this
one sheep. With his blessings, he ✿ could turn one
dish into two, and 100 dishes into 200. There are
numerous narrations to this effect.

We have already looked at another narration
regarding this matter, which occurred with milk
(*laban*). The Prophet ✿ distributed a small pitcher

of milk to Abū Hurayrah ؓ and the rest of the poor members from Ahl al-Ṣuffah. Despite the large number of attendees, the milk never ran out because it came from the blessed hands of the Prophet ﷺ. An even more amazing episode occurred in the Battle of the Trench (al-Khandaq), where more than 1000 people were satiated from the food found in one pot. Once again, the blessing (barakah) came from the Prophet's hand.

In another story, the Prophet ﷺ poured a small amount of water on his hands. He called the Companions to come, as water passed through his fingers in an uninterrupted manner. Because of this continuous supply of water, all of them were able to drink water to their fill and complete the ritual ablution (al-wuḍū'). In fact, the flowing water was so much that they were even able to feed their animals from it as well.

Ultimately, all these examples indicate how the Prophet ﷺ was able to bring forth blessings (barakah) in the quantity of food and drink. From these stories, the scholars have been able to extract a number of benefits and lessons. Perhaps the most important one is that the Prophet ﷺ was exhibiting mercy (raḥmah) through these miracles. This is because through his

love and kindness, the Prophet ﷺ always gives members of his *ummah* more than what they initially expect, whether in this world or the Hereafter.

24

When Jibrīl ﷺ Met Him

Once the Prophet ﷺ became used to receiving revelation from Jibrīl, the fear and intimidation that he felt in the beginning stages of his mission no longer existed. Over time, he ﷺ reached a point where he would long for Jibrīl's arrival, so he could benefit from his presence and receive a new round of revelation from him. In fact, he ﷺ would sometimes ask Jibrīl ﷺ why he would take so long to visit, and if he could come more often. The response for this came from the heavens, as Allah ﷻ has said:

وَمَا نَتَنَزَّلُ إِلَّا بِأَمْرِ رَبِّكَ

"We only descend by the command of your Lord."[13]

---

[13] *al-Maryam*, 64.

In other words, Jibrīl ☙ is not permitted to descend unless if he is explicitly commanded by Allah to do so. Otherwise, he would have visited the Prophet ﷺ far more frequently, as he loved the Prophet ﷺ and the Prophet ﷺ loved him. If you were a person who lived in Madinah during the Prophet's time, you would have known whenever Jibrīl ☙ came to see the Prophet ﷺ. This is because the Messenger of Allah ﷺ would always have a distinct reaction when he saw this honourable angel. This was the case even if no revelation was being given for a particular visit.

During the last ten nights of the month of Ramadan one hopes to be from among those blessed people that will receive the mercy of Allah ☙. Furthermore, during this time, we hope and pray that our houses will be visited by the angels, especially the Chief of the Angels (*sayyid al-malāʾikah*) Jibrīl ☙.

The impact that religiosity is supposed to have on a person's life has been mentioned in the Qur'an, where the following attributes are emphasised:

كَانُوا قَلِيلًا مِنَ اللَّيْلِ مَا يَهْجَعُونَ وَبِالْأَسْحَارِ هُمْ يَسْتَغْفِرُونَ
وَفِي أَمْوَالِهِمْ حَقٌّ لِلسَّائِلِ وَالْمَحْرُومِ

"They used to sleep only little in the night, and pray for forgiveness before dawn, and in their wealth there was a rightful share for the beggar and the poor." [14]

Three key characteristics can be identified from these verses: increasing one's prayer at night, seeking forgiveness, and increasing one's charity. Now, imagine the impact that Jibrīl's visits of the Prophet ﷺ had during Ramadan. It is known that he would visit the Prophet ﷺ every single night of Ramadan. We already know how diligent the Prophet ﷺ was; he would observe the whole night in the performance of voluntary prayers, especially during the last ten nights. But what was his conduct like during the day? On this matter Ibn 'Abbās ﵁ narrates the following report:

كَانَ النَّبِيُّ صَلَّى اللَّهُ عَلَيْهِ وَسَلَّمَ أَجْوَدَ النَّاسِ بِالْخَيْرِ، وَكَانَ أَجْوَدُ مَا يَكُونُ
فِي رَمَضَانَ، حِينَ يَلْقَاهُ جِبْرِيلُ، وَكَانَ جِبْرِيلُ عَلَيْهِ السَّلَامُ يَلْقَاهُ فِي كُلِّ لَيْلَةٍ فِي
رَمَضَانَ حَتَّى يَنْسَلِخَ، يَعْرِضُ عَلَيْهِ النَّبِيُّ صَلَّى اللَّهُ عَلَيْهِ وَسَلَّمَ الْقُرْآنَ

---

[14] *al-Dhāriyāt*, 17-19.

"The Prophet ﷺ was the most generous of all people, and he used to become more generous in Ramadan when Jibrīl met him. Jibrīl ﷺ used to meet him every night to revise the Qur'an with him."

Even more interestingly, Ibn 'Abbās ﷺ notes that when Jibrīl ﷺ met him, yet another change could be observed in the Prophet's behaviour:

فَإِذَا لَقِيَهُ جِبْرِيلُ عَلَيْهِ السَّلاَمُ كَانَ أَجْوَدَ بِالْخَيْرِ مِنَ الرِّيحِ الْمُرْسَلَةِ

"When Jibrīl ﷺ would visit him, he would become more generous than the fast wind (al-rīḥ al-mursalah)."

Let us first analyse the point pertaining to the Prophet's generosity, and what it exactly entails in this context. We can achieve this by bringing up concepts that we have already discussed before. The Prophet ﷺ was the living manifestation of the person who gives charity with their right hand, such that their left hand is totally unaware. This has two different meanings. First, it means that the right hand gives with such openness that the left hand cannot restrain it. Secondly, it means that he ﷺ would give the charity in an extremely sincere manner such that no one else saw it. In fact, the only person who would know of his spending for the sake of Allah was the recipient of the charity itself. In the case of the Prophet ﷺ, everyone benefited from his generosity. Both his hand and heart were so open towards the people that a person could not think that he could increase in generosity. Anas ibn Mālik ﷺ narrated that there was a man who regularly approached the Prophet ﷺ and asked for charity. The Prophet ﷺ gave him so much charity that this man later returned back to his people and said:

يَا قَوْمِ أَسْلِمُوا فَإِنَّ مُحَمَّدًا يُعْطِي عَطَاءً لاَ يَخْشَى الْفَاقَةَ

"O my people! Embrace Islam, for Muhammad gives and does not fear poverty."

One also observes that the Prophet ﷺ exercised this form of generosity for individuals whose hearts needed to be attracted to Islam before they would accept the religion. This type of measure was often needed in the case of the enemies of the Prophet. For instance, in the case of Ṣafwān ibn Umayyah, the Prophet ﷺ gave him 100 camels, and then added a further 100 camels. The Prophet ﷺ gifted him yet another herd of 100 camels, which meant that Ṣafwān was given a grand total of 300 camels. In fact, the Prophet ﷺ had such a generous hand that he would often immediately give in charity any spare wealth or goods he had. This meant that the Prophet's charity distributor Bilāl ﷺ would toil excessively, since he had to ensure that the recipients the Prophet ﷺ had identified received their endowments in a speedy manner. Abū Dharr ﷺ narrates that the

*W*hen the Prophet ﷺ saw Jibrīl ﷻ and accompanied him, that was a form of righteous companionship which inspired him to perform more good deeds. Likewise, the Prophet's own presence had the same inspirational impact on his Companions and community of believers.

Prophet ﷺ said: "If I had gold equal to Mount Uḥud, it would not please me for it to remain with me for more than three days, except an amount which I would keep to repay my debts." As this report indicates, it was his preference to continuously give in charity to anyone who was needy.

ʿUmar ibn al-Khaṭṭāb ﷺ also recounts a beautiful incident, where a man sought charity from the Prophet ﷺ, but the Prophet ﷺ had nothing in his possession to give. Yet the Prophet ﷺ did not want the man to leave empty-handed, so he ordered the man to purchase whatever he wanted, and the Prophet ﷺ would pay his bill. This meant that the Prophet ﷺ was willing to provide this man credit, which he would fully pay off himself in the foreseeable future. ʿUmar ﷺ was troubled by this scene, and did not want to see the Prophet ﷺ be burdened in this manner. He told the Prophet ﷺ: "O Messenger of Allah! I will take care of it. Allah has not burdened you with what is beyond your means." The Prophet ﷺ did not say anything in response, but his facial expression revealed that he did not like what ʿUmar had said. Then a man from the Helpers said:

يَا رَسُولَ اللهِ أَنْفِقْ وَلَا تَخَفْ مِنْ ذِى العَرْشِ إِقْلَالَا

"O Messenger of Allah, give! And do not fear from the Lord of the Throne any type of poverty."

The words of the latter Companion clearly pleased
the Prophet ﷺ, as he began to smile. The Prophet ﷺ
then indicated his agreement with the Helper's words
by saying:

بِهَذَا أُمِرْتُ

"This is what I was commanded to do."

This story indicates that no one could match the
Prophet ﷺ in his openness and generosity, no matter
how much they tried. If someone saw the Prophet ﷺ
in his normal day-to-day routine, they would think
that this was his optimal form of behaviour. But
as the hadiths indicate, when Jibrīl ❀ met him he
would exceed those set standards and become even
more generous. The scholars derived a notable benefit
from this hadith. They mentioned that if you have a
righteous friend or companion in your presence, then
their sight will help you to always remember Allah ﷻ.
This means that you will be more likely to perform
righteous deeds. In the case of the Prophet ﷺ, when
he saw Jibrīl ❀ and accompanied him, that was a
form of righteous companionship which inspired him
to perform more good deeds. Likewise, the Prophet's
own presence had the same inspirational impact on
his Companions and community of believers.

25

Late Night Incidents With Him

A s a Muslim, you would naturally crave for the opportunity to be with the Prophet ﷺ in any time of the day. But during the night, his face would be illuminated in a unique manner, and his guidance would be even more pristine. Consequently, you would love to have the chance to be with the Prophet ﷺ during the night hours; this was a time when the Prophet ﷺ would exert himself by performing more voluntary worship (*ʿibādah*). In addition, during the night many unique conversations occurred between the Prophet ﷺ and the Companions. During this special time and atmosphere, the Prophet ﷺ imparted numerous teachings and reminders to his Companions.

First and foremost, everyone is aware of how the Prophet ﷺ would perform voluntary worship during the last ten nights of Ramadan. As ʿĀʾishah ﷺ narrates:

كَانَ رَسُولُ اللَّهِ صَلَّى اللَّهُ عَلَيْهِ وَسَلَّمَ إِذَا دَخَلَ الْعَشْرُ أَحْيَا اللَّيْلَ وَأَيْقَظَ
أَهْلَهُ وَجَدَّ وَشَدَّ الْمِئْزَرَ

*"When the last ten nights of Ramadan arrived, the
Messenger of Allah would give life to the entire night,
wake up his family, and tighten up his belt."*

The phrase "tighten up his belt" was used to indicate
how serious and diligent he ﷺ became during this
timeframe. In fact, he ﷺ would not sleep at all during
these ten nights. He ﷺ was known to pitch a tent in
the *masjid*, where he would stay and exert himself
in worship for the entirety of that period, regardless
of whether it was the day or night. He ﷺ would
remain in the same spot while remembering Allah
and performing his acts of worship. Ibn 'Umar ﷺ
once drew the attention of Nāfi', and said to him: "By
Allah, this is the exact spot where the Prophet ﷺ used
to pitch his tent and give life to the night."

But these reports did not just discuss his prayer and
other acts of worship. We likewise find many accounts
where the Prophet ﷺ would conduct beautiful and
religious conversations with his Companions. These
types of discussions would occur throughout the year,
and were not simply restricted to the last ten nights of
Ramadan. For instance, Jarīr ibn 'Abdullāh ﷺ stated
that the Messenger of Allah ﷺ came to them on a
night when there was a full moon (*laylah al-badr*).

*T*he Messenger of Allah ﷺ came to his Companions on a night when there was a full moon. He ﷺ then pointed to the moon and said, "You will surely see your Lord on the Day of Judgement just as you see this."

He ﷺ then pointed to the moon and said:

إِنَّكُمْ سَتَرَوْنَ رَبَّكُمْ يَوْمَ القِيَامَةِ كما تَرَوْنَ هذا

"You will surely see your Lord on the Day of Judgement just as you see this."

By this statement, the Prophet ﷺ meant that the believers would have absolutely no difficulty in seeing their Lord in the other world.

Ubayy ibn Ka'b ﷺ says that the Messenger of Allah ﷺ would wake up after one-third of the night had passed to perform the night voluntary prayer (*qiyām*). But what he ﷺ did next. He ﷺ would then call the people and address them with the following words:

يَا أَيُّهَا النَّاسُ اذْكُرُوا اللَّهَ اذْكُرُوا اللَّهَ جَاءَتِ الرَّاجِفَةُ تَتْبَعُهَا الرَّادِفَةُ جَاءَ الْمَوْتُ بِمَا فِيهِ جَاءَ الْمَوْتُ بِمَا فِيهِ

"O people, remember Allah! The first blow of the trumpet has come, and it will then be followed by a second blow. Death has come with all that it comprises."

Through these words, the Prophet ﷺ was reminding the people of how short this life really is. Thus, it is imperative that people focus on the affair of death, even during the night. Note that he ﷺ used to make this address during a normal night. One could only imagine what reminders and admonitions he ﷺ would have issued during the last ten nights of Ramadan. If you were present in Madinah more than 1400 years ago when he ﷺ made this address, what would you have done when you heard these words from your living room? Would you not have been emotionally moved and motivated to pray, while also reflecting on the final moments of your life and how you will return to your Lord?

If you were in the company of the Prophet ﷺ during the night, you would not have left until you witnessed something powerful or miraculous happen to you. Anas ibn Mālik ﷺ describes an amazing incident that involved Usayd ibn Huḍayr and ʿAbbād ibn Bishr ﷺ. As Anas ﷺ mentions, both of these Companions sat with the Prophet ﷺ in a dark night. When they left him, there were two shining lights which accompanied them and illuminated their path. This strongly resembles how the believers will be on the Day of Judgement. When these two Companions parted from one another to reach their respective houses, each one of them had one light in front of them until they safely reached their destinations.

So if you sat and gathered with the Prophet ﷺ, you would have attained some of his spiritual blessings and he would have awakened your heart and soul during the night. The Prophet's heart was always awake, so his beautiful state would enlighten and awaken his audience. But even more amazingly, in some cases you would have actually been blessed with a glittering light that illuminated your path.

If you were blessed to perform worship with the Prophet ﷺ on the Night of Power (*laylah al-qadr*), what was it like? Ibn 'Abbās ﷺ narrates that once the Prophet ﷺ was praying with his Companions on one night of Ramadan. They knew that this night in question was the Night of Power, as the atmosphere was cool and tranquil. They saw the face of the Prophet ﷺ directly prostrate on the mud and water on the ground. During these night prayers, he would also lengthen the duration of his prostration (*sujūd*). The Companions noted that when the Prophet rose up from his prostration, there was mud on his forehead and nose. Tears were also flowing from his eyes. This particular incident occurred on the 23rd night of the month of Ramadan for that year. Of course, the Night of Power is to be sought on all the ten last nights of Ramadan, so a person should perform acts of worship throughout that timeframe.

26

When He Listened to Your Night Prayers

The night prayer (*al-qiyām*) has a unique and eminent status in Islamic society. In fact, Ibn ʿUmar ﷺ stated that it will be the first act of worship to disappear from the Muslim community. Worship in the night consists of two fundamental ingredients: night prayers done after sleep (*tahajjud*), and raising the voice (*rafʿ al-ṣawt*) during recitation. You will find that these two elements played an instrumental role in the success of many heroes of the *ummah*. For instance, in the case of the great fighter Ṣalāḥ al-Dīn al-Ayyūbī ﷺ, it is related that he did not march to Jerusalem until he observed his troops and found them all performing the night prayers. Once he found them busy in the worship of Allah ﷺ during the night hours, he then had the confidence to go and liberate the city. Likewise, the Prophet ﷺ ensured that every household in his community would perform the night prayer on a regular basis.

Obviously, while performing these prayers, you are thinking about the One Who is greater than the Prophet ﷺ and is always watching you: Allah. Likewise, during this act of worship, you have the angels coming around you and blessing you with their presence. But if you were performing the night prayers in the presence of the Prophet ﷺ, what kind of an effect would it have on you?

First and foremost, you would want to listen to his recitation (*qirā'ah*) of the Qur'an. Umm Hāni' said: "I used to sit on my roof and listen to the recitation of the Prophet ﷺ." But most interestingly, the Prophet ﷺ would sometimes go outside and walk in the streets during the night. He would do this in order to listen to the recitation of his Companions without letting them know that he was there. Abū Qatādah ☙ narrated that the Prophet ﷺ went out one night and quietly observed Abū Bakr al-Ṣiddīq ☙ praying in a low voice. Then the Prophet ﷺ went and passed by the house of 'Umar ☙. Of course, 'Umar's voice was deep and loud.

The next day when the Companions met, the Prophet ﷺ provided his assessment of their recitations. He turned to Abū Bakr ☙ and said: "O Abū Bakr, I passed by your house last night, and you were praying in a low voice." Abū Bakr ☙ said in response:

قَدْ أَسْمَعْتُ مَنْ نَاجَيْتُ يَا رَسُولَ اللهِ

"I was able to make the One who I was having an intimate discussion with hear me, O Messenger of Allah."

In essence, Abū Bakr ؓ was pointing to the fact that even if his voice was very low, Allah could still nevertheless hear him. Then the Prophet ﷺ turned to ʿUmar ؓ and said: "When I passed by your house I found your voice to be loud during your prayer." ʿUmar ؓ stated the following in response:

يَا رَسُولَ اللهِ، أُوقِظُ الْوَسْنَانَ، وَأَطْرُدُ الشَّيْطَانَ

"O Messenger of Allah, I wake up the lazy one and expel Shayṭān."

These are the types of responses you would expect from Abū Bakr and ʿUmar ؓ, who had very different character traits but complemented each other well. The Prophet ﷺ then addressed these two Companions by advising them to make a few adjustments. He told Abū Bakr ؓ to raise his voice, while he ordered ʿUmar ؓ to lower the volume of his recitation. This story has some bearing and relation to another incident that occurred close to the end of the Prophet's life. When the Prophet was dying, he appointed Abū Bakr ؓ as the Imam in lieu of him. Interestingly, both ʿĀʾishah and Ḥafṣah ؓ fervently believed that ʿUmar ؓ was a worthier substitute, since his voice was loud and his recitation effectively thwarted the devils (*shayāṭīn*).

There is another story which is likewise related to this theme. 'Ā'ishah narrated that she once returned home late at night after the 'Isha' prayer, and the Prophet ☙ asked her where she was until this moment. 'Ā'ishah responded to the Prophet ☙ by saying: "I was listening to the recitation of one of your Companions. I have never heard a recitation like this before." The Prophet ☙ then suggested that they both go together to listen to him at once. So the Prophet ☙ and 'Ā'ishah both got up and proceeded to the place where this Companion was reciting. As they went to the house that 'Ā'ishah identified and the Prophet could listen to the reciter's voice, it became clear who this Companion was. The Prophet ☙ said:

هَذَا سَالِمٌ مَوْلَى أَبِي حُذَيْفَةَ

"This is Sālim, the freed slave (mawlā) of Abū Ḥudhayfah."

He ☙ then thanked Allah for giving him such a talented reciter in his *ummah* by stating:

الْحَمْدُ لِلّهِ الَّذِي جَعَلَ فِي أُمَّتِي مِثْلَ هَذَا

"Allah praise is due to Allah who has put in my ummah a man like this."

Behold this beautiful testimony. Ask yourself: what kind of assessment would you have likely received if the Prophet ﷺ passed by your house and listened to your recitation?

One will find similar narrations of this nature from the Prophet ﷺ. For instance, Abū Mūsā al-Ashʿarī ؓ narrated that the Prophet ﷺ told him: "If only you had seen me last night! I was standing outside your door, listening to your recitation, and enjoying your voice." Abū Mūsā said: "O Messenger of Allah! Had I known, I would have beautified my voice even further." The Prophet ﷺ then said: "You have been given a sweet voice (*mizmār*) like that of Dāwūd."

Furthermore, there is another beautiful narration in this regard. What makes it my favourite is the fact that it contains a *duʿāʾ* within it as well. ʿUmar ؓ relates that Abū Bakr ؓ, himself, and the Prophet ﷺ had just finished some of their affairs and then proceeded to walk together during the night. They were ultimately walking back to their homes. They happened to pass by the house of ʿAbdullāh ibn Masʿūd ؓ, who was one of the main reciters and scribes of the Prophet ﷺ. He was one of the eminent Companions who held the distinction of learning the Qurʾan directly from the mouth of the Prophet ﷺ. Once they reached his house, the Prophet stopped, and so Abū Bakr and ʿUmar

The Prophet ﷺ told Abū Mūsā al-Ashʿarī ﷺ: "If only you had seen me last night! I was standing outside your door, listening to your recitation, and enjoying your voice." Abū Mūsā said: "O Messenger of Allah! Had I known, I would have beautified my voice even further."

remained put as well. The reason for this was because Ibn Masʿūd ﷺ was beautifully reciting the Qur'an.

Recall that Ibn Masʿūd ﷺ was the very same Companion who caused the Prophet ﷺ to cry after reciting *Surah al-Nisā'* in his presence. In that case, the Prophet ﷺ had personally asked Ibn Masʿūd ﷺ to read in front of him. But in this scenario, Ibn Masʿūd was totally unaware that the Prophet ﷺ, Abū Bakr, and ʿUmar ﷺ were outside of his door. The Prophet ﷺ stood motionless, carefully listening to the recitation from inside the house. Ibn Masʿūd ﷺ finished his recitation in the prayer, where he then bowed (*rukūʿ*) and prostrated (*sujūd*) afterwards. Once he concluded the prayer, they knew that he would then proceed to making a *duʿā'* as well. At this point, the Prophet ﷺ remarked: "Proceed and ask what you wish, for you will be given it." In his supplication, Ibn Masʿūd said:

اللَّهُمَّ إِنِّي أَسْأَلُكَ إِيمَانًا لَا يَرْتَدُّ، وَنَعِيمًا لَا يَنْفَدُ، وَمُرَافَقَةَ مُحَمَّدٍ صَلَّى اللهُ
عَلَيْهِ وَسَلَّمَ فِي أَعْلَى جَنَّةِ الْخُلْدِ

"O Allah, I ask of you for faith that is not taken away, for blessings that do not expire, and the companionship of the Prophet in the Highest Eternal Garden (Jannah al-Firdaws)."

After Ibn Masʿūd ﷺ finished, the Prophet ﷺ asked Allah to accept his *duʿā'* by saying āmīn. The next day ʿUmar ؓ was extremely excited and went to Ibn Masʿūd ؓ, seeking to inform him that the Prophet ﷺ had listened and blessed his *duʿā'* by asking Allah to accept it. However, Ibn Masʿūd said: "Abū Bakr already beat you to it." ʿUmar was stunned and said: "*Subḥānallāh*, there is no good deed except that Abū Bakr beats me in performing it."

The Most Amazing Thing About Him

May Allah be pleased with our Mother 'Ā'ishah 🌸.
She is one of the primary sources who provided
us numerous glimpses of the life of the Prophet ﷺ
through the thousands of narrations she related. In
addition, she provided so many touching details of
the interactions she had with the Prophet ﷺ, such as
any arguments, jokes, and life moments they had with
one another. These are aspects which we do not alone
appreciate or aspire to hear. In actual fact, even the
Companions wanted to sit with her and hear about
these beautiful details of her life experiences with the
Prophet ﷺ. It was important for them to know how
the Prophet ﷺ was like in his home, and when he was
alone with his family. These types of questions were
particularly important for the next generation—the
Successors (Tābi'ūn)—who never had the chance to
see the Prophet ﷺ. They would visit and sit with her,

while asking her direct questions concerning the Prophet's conduct in his private quarters. When we are interacting and analysing the narrations that follow, try to imagine yourself being in the presence of ʿĀʾishah 🌼.

In reality, one could never get enough information on this matter from ʿĀʾishah 🌼. On the one hand, the believers wanted to know the human dimension of the Prophet 🌼. While on the other, they wanted to know the superhuman elements that he was endowed with as a Messenger of Allah. It is important to note that when the people asked her "What was he like?" they actually had a specific meaning in mind. By this they meant whether the Prophet 🌼 rested and took breaks in his daily life, just like how other humans do. Did he become fatigued and tired like others after spending a busy day at work? In response to such queries, ʿĀʾishah 🌼 made it abundantly clear that the Prophet 🌼 was a normal human being just like others. When he would come home, he would clean his clothing by removing any lice from it and milk the goats. He actively served his family by performing many of the household tasks and chores. He would feed the cattle that he owned, and would tie his camel. He would eat with the slaves, and help them in their work such as kneading the dough. In fact, he would carry and bring his own groceries. ʿĀʾishah 🌼

enumerated the contributions of the Prophet in the household by saying:

$$كَانَ يَكُونُ فِي مِهْنَةِ أَهْلِهِ$$

"He was constantly in the service of his family."

She ﷺ also noted that the Prophet ﷺ would frequently joke inside the house. Many of his jokes which have reached us actually were said to her directly, in order to make her smile and bring happiness in the household. In ʿĀʾishah's narrations there is always an amazing attention to detail regarding the interactions that the Prophet ﷺ had with his family and with his guests. For example, she noted that the Prophet ﷺ would ask her what part of the glass she drank from. After indicating to him the exact spot, he would drink from that place as well. ʿĀʾishah ﷺ would smile and sometimes even laugh when relating that the Prophet ﷺ would kiss her. That was because recalling such memories would make her emotional, as those moments used to bring her intense happiness. She also recalled how the Prophet ﷺ would personally serve his guests when they visited his home. The Prophet ﷺ was never a passive or idle actor inside the house perimeter; instead, regardless of the day or circumstance, he would play an active and productive role. What made him special was that he would give his family everything that he possibly could.

In addition, this level of productivity was always found on a consistent basis; there were no lapses on his part. Taking these facts into consideration, it is thus no surprise that upon being asked about the Prophet's character, 'Ā'ishah ﷺ produced the following answer:

كَانَ خُلُقُهُ الْقُرْآنَ

"His character was that of the Qur'an."

That is the greatest form of praise that she gave him among her narrations. In essence, whatever the Prophet ﷺ taught to his followers, he embodied it as well. In another narration, she said:

اِقْرَأْ قَدْ أَفْلَحَ الْمُؤْمِنُونَ. قَالَ يَزِيدُ فَقَرَأْتُ قَدْ أَفْلَحَ الْمُؤْمِنُونَ إِلَى لِفُرُوجِهِمْ حَافِظُونَ، قَالَتْ: هَكَذَا كَانَ خُلُقُ رَسُولِ اللهِ صَلَّى اللهُ عَلَيْهِ وَسَلَّمَ

"Read if you wish, 'Successful indeed are the believers' up to 'those who guard their chastity'.[15] *That was the character of the Messenger of Allah ﷺ."*

When asked about his worship, 'Ā'ishah ﷺ produced an equally beautiful answer. She noted that as beautiful as his worship was from the outside realm, the inner aspects of his acts of obedience reached an unimaginable degree of splendour. She was asked

---

[15] *al-Mu'minūn*, 1-5.

about his night prayer (*qiyām*), particularly during the month of Ramadan. In response, she stated that the Messenger of Allah ﷺ used to pray a total of eleven *rak'ahs*, both during and outside of Ramadan. He would achieve this grand total by offering two four *rak'ah* cycles, which were then followed by three *rak'ahs* Witr prayer. Then she spoke about the quality of his night prayer by saying: "Do not ask me about their beauty and length." This is because no one else's prayer could match his in terms of tranquility and serenity. So she gave special emphasis to the Prophet's night prayer, and its unparalleled beauty. 'Ā'ishah ﷺ also notes that she once asked the Prophet ﷺ whether he would sleep before performing his Witr prayer. In response, the Prophet ﷺ said:

يَا عَائِشَةُ إِنَّ عَيْنَيَّ تَنَامَانِ وَلَا يَنَامُ قَلْبِي

"O 'Ā'ishah, my eyes sleep, but my heart remains awake."

His heart would never sleep. A parallel to this can be found in how the Prophet ﷺ would welcome the sound of the call of prayer (*adhān*) and find relief and happiness in it. He would say to Bilāl ﷺ:

أَرِحْنَا بِهَا يَا بِلَالُ

"Comfort us with it, O Bilāl."

During the night, he was likewise eager to serve his Lord by praying to Him inside his home. The Prophet's intimate and consistent relationship with his Lord was what his family noted the most. Within this context, there is a powerful narration which continues to amaze and stun me. I want you to imagine that you are currently in the presence of our Mother ʿĀʾishah ﵂, and you collected from her all of the aforementioned narrations. But now you ask her to share with you the most incredible and amazing thing she saw from the Prophet ﷺ. If she could identify the best experience she shared with him, what would it be? This very question was posed to her, and upon hearing it, she became silent and started to cry (*sakatat wa bakat*). After crying for a long period of time, she then proceeded to provide a comprehensive answer. First and foremost, she noted that:

$$كَانَ كُلُّ أَمْرِهِ عَجَباً$$

"Everything about him was amazing."

Everything regarding his affairs and how he carried himself as a Prophet was amazing, without there being any exceptions. But she then noted that the events found on one particular night were the most amazing. On this night the Prophet ﷺ came to bed and rested right beside ʿĀʾishah ﵂, such that his skin made contact with hers. He then said to her:

Aishah ﷺ said about the Prophet ﷺ that "His character was that of the Qur'an." When she ﷺ was asked to identify the best experience she shared with him ﷺ, she became silent and cried for a long period of time and then began by saying, "Everything about him was amazing."

"O ʿĀʾishah, will you permit me to go and worship my Lord tonight?" He sought her permission before leaving the bed and commencing his worship! This was during the early parts of the night, where the Prophet ﷺ would usually rest and sleep before waking up to pray during the night hours. Here he was, gently snuggling with his wife, before asking her if she approved of his departure. In response to his request, ʿĀʾishah ﷺ said:

وَاللهِ، إِنِّي لَأُحِبُّ قُرْبَكَ، وَأُحِبُّ مَا يَسُرُّكَ

"By Allah, I love being close to you, but I also love what makes you happy."

Essentially, she was telling him that despite loving his presence, she loved what pleased him. So if he wanted to go and pray early in the night, she would be content with that. ʿĀʾishah ﷺ remained on the bed, and observed what the Prophet ﷺ did next. She notes that the Prophet ﷺ rose up and performed his ablution, then made the opening *takbīr*, and then commenced his prayer. But then she adds that the Prophet ﷺ wept so much that his beard became wet from his tears. ʿĀʾishah ﷺ had seen the Prophet's night prayer for years. We all know, for instance, how frequently the Prophet ﷺ would perform the night prayers in this small room, as he used to tap ʿĀʾishah ﷺ so she could move up her legs.

But this particular night was unusually different. The Prophet ﷺ was weeping so much that he soaked both his beard and his place of prayer with tears. The ground and 'Ā'ishah's feet became wet with tears. At this point, 'Ā'ishah ﷺ became concerned and feared something might be wrong. Had something bad happened to the Prophet ﷺ which caused him to cry in this emotional manner? Since she was a good and dutiful wife, 'Ā'ishah ﷺ sought to investigate the matter. She approached the Prophet ﷺ and said: "O Messenger of Allah, why are you crying so much?" She then tried to sooth him with the following words:

لِمَ تَصْنَعُ هَذَا يَا رَسُولَ اللَّهِ وَقَدْ غَفَرَ اللَّهُ لَكَ مَا تَقَدَّمَ مِنْ ذَنْبِكَ وَمَا تَأَخَّرَ

"Why do you do this, O Messenger of Allah, while Allah has forgiven you for everything you have done in the past and everything that will follow?"

The Prophet ﷺ looked at 'Ā'ishah ﷺ and gave this moving response:

أَفَلَا أَكُونُ عَبْدًا شَكُورًا؟ لَقَدْ أُنْزِلَتْ عَلَيَّ اللَّيْلَةَ آيَةٌ وَيْلٌ لِمَنْ قَرَأَهَا وَلَمْ يَتَفَكَّرْ فِيهَا

"Shall I not be a grateful servant? Verily on this night a verse (āyah) was revealed to me. Woe to the one who reads but does not ponder over it."

The verse which the Prophet 🌸 was referring to was the following:

إِنَّ فِي خَلْقِ السَّمَاوَاتِ وَالأَرْضِ وَاخْتِلَافِ اللَّيْلِ وَالنَّهَارِ وَالْفُلْكِ الَّتِي تَجْرِي فِي الْبَحْرِ بِمَا يَنفَعُ النَّاسَ وَمَا أَنزَلَ اللهُ مِنَ السَّمَاءِ مِن مَّاءٍ فَأَحْيَا بِهِ الأَرْضَ بَعْدَ مَوْتِهَا وَبَثَّ فِيهَا مِن كُلِّ دَآبَّةٍ وَتَصْرِيفِ الرِّيَاحِ وَالسَّحَابِ الْمُسَخِّرِ بَيْنَ السَّمَاءِ وَالأَرْضِ لَآيَاتٍ لِقَوْمٍ يَعْقِلُونَ

"Indeed, in the creation of the heavens and the earth; the alternation of the day and the night; the ships that sail the sea for the benefit of humanity; the rain sent down by Allah from the skies, reviving the earth after its death; the scattering of all kinds of creatures throughout; the shifting of the winds; and the clouds drifting between the heavens and the earth—are surely signs for people of understanding."[16]

ʿĀʾishah 🌸 witnessed a manifest evidence of Allah's existence and the truth of this religion right in front of her eyes. That manifest proof was none other than the Prophet 🌸, who was crying due to the signs that Allah 🌸 has left for us, all of which indicate His existence. Should we then not be from the people of understanding, and reflect as well?

---

[16] *al-Baqarah*, 164.

When He Prayed for Us

Even if you were not present in the room with him, you were nevertheless still in the heart of the Prophet ﷺ. The *ummah* in its entirety was included in the *du'ā'* of the Prophet ﷺ, regardless of whether you lived in his time period or not. There are so many occasions where the Prophet ﷺ prayed for us without us even hearing his words. But there were others who heard his supplications and transmitted them to us.

'Ā'ishah ﷺ mentions that on one certain night, the Prophet ﷺ was not lying in bed next to her. So she started looking for him. Because it was dark, she started moving her hand around to see if she could make contact with the Prophet ﷺ; eventually her hand landed on his foot. Because his foot was upright, it meant that the Prophet ﷺ was in the position of prostration (*sajdah*). She then heard the Messenger of Allah ❀ recite the following:

اللَّهُمَّ إِنِّي أَعُوذُ بِرِضَاكَ مِنْ سَخَطِكَ وَبِمُعَافَاتِكَ مِنْ عُقُوبَتِكَ، وَأَعُوذُ
بِكَ مِنْكَ، لَا أُحْصِي ثَنَاءً عَلَيْكَ أَنْتَ كَمَا أَثْنَيْتَ عَلَى نَفْسِكَ

"O Allah, I seek refuge in Your pleasure from your anger, and I seek refuge in Your forgiveness from your punishment. And I seek refuge in You from you. And I cannot praise You as you have praised Yourself."

This is a very famous *du'ā'* which we should aim to recite every single night, if possible. The meaning of this last sentence is that one's praise for Allah ❀ will always be deficient; His praise for Himself will only be sufficient.

This was the Prophet's prayer during his prostration. He ❀ would supplicate so much that we cannot accurately capture how many of those *du'ā*'s were for himself, and how many were for his *ummah.* But there were essential traits and consistent themes found for every occasion he made *du'ā*', regardless of whether it was indoors or at the *masjid.* For one thing, he would take his time when supplicating to his Lord. In fact, on one occasion, he remained in a state of prostration for so long that the Companions actually feared that he was dead. One could only imagine for how long he was still and motionless for these onlookers to have this false impression. Yet, this was the case when the Prophet ﷺ prostrated to his Lord.

When they asked the Prophet ﷺ what had happened, he raised his head in a mournful and weeping state. At that moment, Jibrīl ﷺ descended and asked him: "Allah has sent me to see why you are crying." The Prophet ﷺ said in response:

اللَّهُمَّ أُمَّتِي أُمَّتِي

"O Allah, my ummah, my ummah."

Allah ﷻ then sent down Jibrīl ﷺ and ordered him to say in response:

إِنَّا سَنُرْضِيكَ فِي أُمَّتِكَ وَلَا نَسُوؤُكَ

"We will please you with your ummah, and we will never disappoint you."

This particular incident happened outside his house. But there were notable scenarios that occurred inside his residence as well. For the latter, 'Ā'ishah ﷺ relates that on one night, the Prophet ﷺ stood up in prayer and was continuously repeating a single verse over and over again. Umm Salamah ﷺ and Abū Dharr ﷺ relate similar narrations to this effect. They stated that the Prophet ﷺ spent the entire night reciting the following verse:

إِن تُعَذِّبْهُمْ فَإِنَّهُمْ عِبَادُكَ ۖ وَإِن تَغْفِرْ لَهُمْ فَإِنَّكَ أَنتَ الْعَزِيزُ الْحَكِيمُ

"If You punish them, they belong to You after all.
But if You forgive them, You are surely the Almighty,
All-Wise." [17]

Furthermore, it is well established that the Prophet ﷺ
would make *du'ā'* for us—his *ummah*—throughout
the entire night. The most beautiful narration in this
regard comes from 'Ā'ishah, who stated that she once
noticed that the Prophet ﷺ was in a particularly good
mood. As we have already established before, 'Ā'ishah ﷺ
knew very well of the power of the Prophet's *du'ā'*
and his miracles. Naturally, if you noticed that the
Prophet ﷺ was in a splendid mood like this, you
would take advantage of the opportunity and ask
for his *du'ā'*. Would you not do the same thing if the
Prophet ﷺ was inside your house and present before
you? You definitely would have asked him to do so.
This is in fact what 'Ā'ishah ﷺ did. She said to the
Prophet ﷺ: "O Messenger of Allah, make *du'ā'* for
me." The Prophet ﷺ responded positively to her
request by raising his hands and saying:

اللَّهُمَّ اغْفِرْ لِعَائِشَةَ مَا تَقَدَّمَ مِن ذَنِبهَا وَمَا تَأَخَّرَ، مَا أَسَرَّتْ وَمَا أَعْلَنَتْ

"O Allah, forgive all of 'Ā'ishah's sins: the previous and
the future ones, the secret ones and the future ones."

---

[17] *al-Mā'idah*, 118.

Subḥānallāh, what an invocation! One cannot fail to notice that this *duʿāʾ* is similar in wording to what ʿĀishah ﷻ mentioned to the Prophet ﷺ after she saw him crying in his prayer. The Prophet ﷺ explained to her that he was being grateful after she mentioned to him that Allah had forgiven him for all his sins. Upon hearing this beautiful and comprehensive invocation, ʿĀishah ﷻ become extremely pleased, and laughed so much that her head dropped on the lap of the Prophet ﷺ. Think of this scene: ʿĀishah ﷻ is laughing in joy and rests on the lap of the Prophet ﷺ. The Prophet ﷺ then asked ʿĀishah ﷻ: "Has my *duʿāʾ* pleased you?" She stated in response: "And how can your *duʿāʾ* not please me?" The Prophet ﷺ then stated:

وَاللَّهِ إِنَّهَا لَدُعَائِي لِأُمَّتِي فِي كُلِّ صَلَاةٍ

"I swear by Allah, this is the duʿāʾ that I make for my entire ummah in every single prayer."

Even if you were not present in the room with him, you were nevertheless still in the heart of the Prophet ﷺ. It is well established that the Prophet ﷺ would make du'ā' for us—his ummah—throughout the entire night.

The Pain
of His Death

All the principles and axioms that we know regarding death apply the most to the Prophet ﷺ. One of these key principles is that when a person dies, either they are relieved of this world or the world is relieved of them. When Allah ﷻ speaks about an evil person, He says:

فَمَا بَكَتْ عَلَيْهِمُ السَّمَاءُ وَالأَرْضُ

"Neither heaven nor earth wept over them." [18]

As for the righteous person, Ibn 'Abbās ﷺ mentions that when they die, the heavens cry when they leave this world. This is because the gate of the heavens which their good deeds used to pass through is no longer open. Likewise, their place of prostration

---

[18] *al-Dukhān*, 29.

(*sajdah*) on the earth weeps as well. Now, reflect on the eminence of the Prophet 🌸 in that regard. He was a person that everyone and everything longed for when he was alive. Likewise, everyone and everything mourned his death after he left this world.

If you lived in Madinah more than 1400 years ago, your entire life revolved around the Prophet 🌸. For every single moment of your life, you would have thought about what he was doing. Your goal would have been to obtain his desire and become one of his Companions. For more than a decade, members of civil society in Madinah engaged themselves in this way vis-à-vis the Prophet 🌸. This is because the day the Prophet 🌸 migrated to Madinah, it was like the birth of a newborn; a new light illuminated the city and gave it a completely unprecedented meaning.

There is a vivid scene during the Battle of Uḥud which encapsulates this point well. During the conflict someone shouted that the Prophet 🌸 was killed during the conflict. Upon hearing this, the Companions immediately put down their weapons and armour and began to cry. They ceased fighting, as they felt that there was no longer any reason for them to live without the Prophet 🌸. One should note that they had this deep attachment with the Prophet 🌸 despite having known him for only just a few years. Now fast forward many years later, where the Companions are sitting quietly in the *masjid* in a state of deep anxiety, and asking themselves whether they will see the Prophet ﷺ recover from the illness he suffered from at the end of his life. Many of the Companions had this deep inner feeling that the Prophet ﷺ was going to live, and that he would somehow recuperate his strength. It was inevitable that he would come out of this. The Companions knew that the Prophet ﷺ was a human being, but they could not imagine that he would actually die. Considering the number of people that he healed over the years and cured through his *duʿāʾ*, they could not imagine that he would depart from this world so soon. He had saved the lives of countless individuals during the course of his prophethood. Thus, they believed that the Prophet ﷺ would overcome his illness and continue to live.

What provides a beautiful sense of closure is that the last recorded sighting of the Prophet ﷺ was a beautiful smile. Anas ؓ describes the final moments of the Prophet's life while he was inside his room. They said that during one of their prayers, the Prophet ﷺ drew his curtain. And then he gave the Companions a wide smile, where all his teeth could be seen. They described his face as resembling the page of a *muṣḥaf*, which was an allusion to the pristine beauty found in his face during his last moment. It was also a reference to the fact that his most beautiful smile was actually displayed at the end of his life. Upon migrating to Madinah, there were some Companions who embraced Islam due to his smile, such as ʿAbdullāh ibn Salām ﷺ. Now he was going to leave the city of Madinah with a smile as well.

When the Companions were in prayer, they actually had their spirits lifted because the way he was smiling was interpreted as a sign that he would have a full recovery and preside over his duties again. The Prophet ﷺ addressed them by saying: "Keep on praying." This can be interpreted as meaning: "Keep on going." It was as if the Prophet ﷺ was telling them that he had fulfilled his duty and conveyed his message, and now it was upon the Companions to continue acting upon his teachings. Then he closed the curtains and returned to his room. At this point, the Companions that were in the *masjid* became very anxious, as the Prophet's condition was not actually stabilising. Unlike in the past, it was not ʿĀ'ishah's head which was resting on the Prophet's lap. Instead, the Prophet's head was resting on ʿĀ'ishah's lap.

*U*nable to attend the prayer in his final illness, the last recorded sighting of the Prophet ﷺ was a beautiful smile. He ﷺ addressed them by saying: "Keep on praying." It was as if the Prophet ﷺ was telling them to "keep on going." He had fulfilled his duty and conveyed his message, and now it was upon the Companions to continue acting upon his teachings.

'Ā'ishah 🙵 vividly described the severity of the fever which the Prophet 🙵 suffered from, and mentioned that while undergoing pain, the Prophet 🙵 would say:

$$\text{لَا إِلَهَ إِلَّا اللهُ، إِنَّ لِلْمَوْتِ سَكَرَاتٍ}$$

"There is no god but Allah. Indeed, the coming of death is difficult."

Through these words, the Prophet 🙵 was indicating to us the fact that the last moments of life are difficult. Ibn Masʿūd 🙵 mentioned that the fever of the Prophet 🙵 was hotter than anything he had felt in his life. While the Prophet 🙵 was on the lap of his wife, he noticed that 'Ā'ishah's brother ʿAbd al-Raḥmān 🙵 had a tooth-stick (*siwāk*) in his hand. 'Ā'ishah 🙵 realised that the Prophet 🙵 was looking at it, so she asked the Prophet 🙵: "Would you like me to bring it to you?" The Prophet 🙵 nodded his head affirmatively. So 'Ā'ishah 🙵 took the tooth-stick, chewed it a bit, and then gave it to the Prophet 🙵, so he could use it. The Prophet 🙵 then used the tooth-stick to clean his blessed teeth for the very last time of his life. He was known to use the tooth-stick for every single prayer of the day and night, so his mouth would be clean and fresh before conversing with his Lord.

While he was using the tooth-stick, he looked up. His face lit up as Jibrīl 🙵 entered the room. At that point,

Jibrīl ﷺ said that the Prophet ﷺ had one of two choices. First, if he wished, he could live for eternity, that is, as long as this world existed. Or he could opt to depart from this world and be with the Highest Companion (*al-Rafīq al-Aʿlā*). The Prophet ﷺ almost immediately indicated his choice of being with Allah, the Highest Companion. He continued to emphasise his choice by looking up and saying repeatedly: "I choose the Highest Companion." ʿĀʾishah ﷺ mentioned that the Prophet continued saying this until his blessed hand came down and his soul left his body. She said that immediately afterwards, a beautiful scent filled the entire room. It is known that when the righteous soul is being taken away, the angels come with a shroud that is saturated with perfume. Undoubtedly, the angels that came to take the Prophet's soul had brought with them a shroud containing the best of scents and fragrances. The Companions noted that this was the most beautiful scent that they had ever smelled in their lives. While this all happened, ʿĀʾishah ﷺ began to cry and shout.

Imagine if you were inside the *masjid* on that fateful day, sitting down and quietly worshipping Allah. But then suddenly you hear the cries and shouts of ʿĀʾishah ﷺ. Afterwards, you hear people from the Prophet's room saying:

مَاتَ رَسُولُ اللهِ! مَاتَ رَسُولُ اللهِ! مَاتَ رَسُولُ اللهِ!

*"The Messenger of Allah has died! The Messenger of
Allah has died! The Messenger of Allah has died!"*

You are now totally shocked, and your whole body
has become numb. You now stare at the curtain of
the room and ask yourself whether the Prophet ﷺ
would open it again and address his people with a
reminder, or simply give a smile. You will definitely
ask yourself whether the whole claim is a hoax, just
like what happened in the Battle of Uḥud. During
that conflict, there were numerous people who
thought that the Prophet ﷺ had died, yet that claim
turned out to be false. Perhaps the same thing has
occurred for this latest episode.

Everybody was in a state of shock and disbelief.
People were looking at one another, hoping to
receive some form of logical explanation for how
the Prophet ﷺ could still be alive. People looked at
the curtain and expected the Prophet ﷺ to appear
from behind it. Over time, some of the Companions
began to come to terms with this event and accepted
what had happened. ʿAlī ﷺ, who was unrivalled in
his eloquence, was so stunned that he could not say
a word. ʿUthmān ﷺ was so shocked that he could
not even stand up. ʿUmar ﷺ had become so upset
that he harshly rebuked anyone who claimed that

the Messenger of Allah ﷺ had died, and dismissed them as being liars and individuals who were stirring dissension (*fitnah*) in the community. In his view, the Prophet ﷺ could not be dead, and anyone who claimed otherwise was a hypocrite. He obviously could not come to terms with this reality. The short sentence "The Messenger of Allah has died" stung every person who was inside the *masjid* that day. During this state of turmoil and confusion, Abū Bakr ﷺ stood up and addressed everyone by saying:

مَن كَانَ مِنكُم يَعْبُدُ مُحَمَّدًا صَلَّى اللهُ عَلَيْهِ وَسَلَّمَ، فَإِنَّ مُحَمَّدًا قدْ مَاتَ،
وَمَن كَانَ مِنكُم يَعْبُدُ اللهَ فَإِنَّ اللهَ حَيٌّ لَا يَمُوتُ

"Whoever among you used to worship Muhammad,
then Muhammad is dead. And whoever used to
worship Allah, then Allah is alive and ever-living."

The prevailing sentiment among everyone on that day was one of immense sadness and grief. Imagine an entire community, where a child of every family dies at the same time. That would definitely be an immense tragedy. However, what happened on that day was far more worse and painful, since the person who departed and left them was the most beloved person in the heart of every believer. They had to come to terms with that giant loss in every area of their lives. They would have to go to their houses, only to then remember the times the Prophet ﷺ visited them as a guest. They had to pray in the *masjid*, while no longer being able to listen to his recitation. They had to celebrate and participate in times of joy, but without the comfort and smile of the Prophet ﷺ. This ultimately meant that every single occasion would now have its pain and discomfort.

The death of the Prophet ﷺ does have an indirect relation with the pain of losing a child. There is a hadith where the Prophet ﷺ spoke of the rewards for the ones who lose a child in their lives. At this point, one of the Companions asked: "O Messenger of Allah! What about those individuals from your *ummah* who will not be afflicted with the loss of a child?" He ﷺ said in response:

فَأَنَا فَرَطٌ لأُمَّتِي، لَنْ يُصَابُوا بِمِثْلِي

*"Then I am the loss for my ummah, for they will not
be afflicted with a loss like mine."*

30

Longing for
His Presence

The Prophet ﷺ said: "There are people from my *ummah* who will come after me, yet they will love me so much that they would give up their families and wealth in exchange for simply seeing me."

Undoubtedly, there is a feeling of pain and emptiness that many of us may experience since we have not had the opportunity to see the Prophet ﷺ. Yet, it is amazing to know that the Prophet ﷺ had an affinity towards us whenever he would visit the graveyards.

He would go to al-Baqīʿ cemetery and visit the graves of those who had passed before him. But during that setting, he ﷺ said:

وَدِدْتُ أَنْ لَوْ رَأَيْتُ إِخْوَانِي

"I wish I could meet my brothers."

The Companions were surprised to hear this statement
from the Prophet ☙, especially since it was uttered
in the graveyard. It was not clear to them who he
was referring to in this statement. Was he talking
about the people who had already passed away or
the current Companions? So they ultimately said: "O
Messenger of Allah, are we not your brothers?" The
Prophet ☙ said in response:

بَلْ أَنْتُمْ أَصْحَابِي وَلَكِنْ إِخْوَانِي الَّذِينَ آمَنُوا بِي وَلَمْ يَرَوْنِي

*"No, you are my Companions. I am referring to my
brothers who will believe in me despite not seeing me."*

If you had the opportunity to see him, things would
have been substantially different. Even if you saw him
in a dream and witnessed his blessed face, then you
would be constantly longing for him. Those who are
not blessed with such a sight have to constantly push
themselves to connect with him. The Prophet ☙ was
aware of how much the later generations would want
to see him. He likewise wished to see them. Even the
Companions who saw and corresponded with the
Prophet ☙ on a daily basis had great fears that even if
they made it to Paradise, they might not be able to see
the Prophet ☙ anymore.

'Ā'ishah ☙ narrated that a young man once came to
the Prophet ☙ while he was weeping. The Prophet

said to him: "What is causing you to cry?" The young man said: "Every day that I wake up, I look forward to seeing you. If I wish to see you, I simply go to the *masjid*. But I remember that there will be a day where I will die." The man had lofty manners (*adab*) with the Prophet ﷺ, such that he mentioned his own death, not the Prophet's. This was despite the fact that the Prophet ﷺ was older than him; nevertheless, he mentioned his own death. He then said: "Even if I enter Paradise, where will you be, and where will I be?" The Prophet ﷺ said:

$$أَنْتَ مَعَ مَنْ أَحْبَبْتَ$$

"You are with the one you love."

The Prophet ﷺ knew that his narrations would be recorded and transmitted, so he ensured that the later generations would become aware that they would certainly meet on the Day of Judgement. He emphasised the fact that the later generations of his *ummah* would face greater trials and difficulties. But he noted that on the Day of Judgement, he will be waiting by the Pool (Ḥawḍ) for them to come with a cup in his hand. He will ensure that all the generations of his *ummah* would be able to drink directly from his blessed hand. Longing for that moment is in fact an act of worship. Al-Ḥasan al-Baṣrī ؓ once said:

يَا مَعْشَرَ الْمُسْلِمِينَ الْخَشَبَةُ تَحِنُّ إِلَى رَسُولِ اللهِ صَلَّى اللهُ عَلَيْهِ وَسَلَّمَ
شَوْقاً إِلَى لِقَائِهِ فَأَنْتُمْ أَحَقُّ أَنْ تَشْتَاقُوا إِلَيْهِ

"O servants of Allah! The stump of the date-palm tree
yearned for the Messenger of Allah ❀. You should
thus have a greater yearning to meet him."

In addition, if we get into Paradise, we will personally
be able to have the moments, experiences, and
interactions that we missed enjoying in this world.
Everything that we wished to do with him in this
world will become possible in the next life. For
instance, in Paradise every single Friday is considered
a day of Eid, where celebrations, gatherings, and
festivities will be held. On Fridays, one will thus have
the chance to meet the Prophet ❀ on a weekly basis.
In fact, for that day of the week, the believers will
have the opportunity to see the One Who is greater
than the Prophet ❀, and that is Allah ❀ Himself.

In Paradise, everything with the Prophet ❀ will
become possible. If you missed seeing his smile in this
life, you will be able to witness his smile and laugh in
Paradise as much as you want. If you were unable to
hear his voice and conduct a conversation with him in
this world, you will be able to interact with him in the
other world. Even hosting him in your own house will
become a possibility, where he can see your family
and children. Likewise, should you wish, you could

have him share many of his personal stories about himself and his family members which never reached the compiled works.

But for this dream to be realised, you must long for that and exert efforts in the attainment of that goal. The Prophet ﷺ has taught us that there are two essential ingredients which will allow us to meet him in the Hereafter. The first is purity of creed, which comprises of the aspects of faith which make us Muslims in the first place. But what gets us closest to him in Paradise is good character. You must make an active effort to adopt and implement all the Prophetic character traits that you have read about him. You must constantly attempt to bring the Prophet's code of conduct into your life. By doing so, you will remember him throughout your life, and ultimately long for him. By longing for him more, you will have the tendency to send more blessings (*ṣalawāt*) upon him. Once you begin doing this, you will develop an intricate connection with the Prophet ﷺ. Every time you send salutations upon him by saying, "O Allah! Send blessings upon Muhammad (*Allāhumma ṣalli ʿalā Muḥammad*)", he will respond to you. Even though you have never met him, you will receive his *duʿā'* and love.

O Allah! Send blessings upon Prophet Muhammad. May our hearts always be inclined to remember him and long for him. Let our love for him drive us to make an active effort to adopt and implement all the Prophetic character traits that we have learned about. O Allah, allow us to meet our beloved Prophet ﷺ in Paradise.

Āmīn.

May the peace
and blessings of Allah
be upon him.